IMAGES
of America

NEW MEXICO'S
RANGERS
THE MOUNTED POLICE

IMAGES
of America

NEW MEXICO'S
RANGERS
THE MOUNTED POLICE

Chuck Hornung

ARCADIA
PUBLISHING

Published by Arcadia Publishing
Charleston, South Carolina

Printed in the United States of America

Library of Congress Control Number: 2010923454

For all general information contact Arcadia Publishing at:
Telephone 843-853-2070
Fax 843-853-0044
E-mail sales@arcadiapublishing.com
For customer service and orders:
Toll-Free 1-888-313-2665

Visit us on the Internet at www.arcadiapublishing.com

"To the man who trailed the desert foot-by-foot and piece-by-piece, the lad they called Kid Lambert of the New Mexico Mounted Police."

—*Charles Frederick Lambert*
January 23, 1887–February 3, 1971

CONTENTS

FOREWORD

The New Mexico Mounted Police has a certain ring to the name, but growing up in New Mexico I had never heard of this organization of frontier lawmen. I had not been a New Mexico State Police officer very long when in 1976, the New Mexico State Police Association published an annual featuring all the current officer's photographs and a history of the state police. On page 64 of the annual, there were four photographs and three paragraphs that told a simple history of the mounted police. At that point in my career such a small sample of the history of a pre-statehood law enforcement organization did not interest me.

However, four years later I developed an interest in the history of the New Mexico State Police and started collecting photographs and memorabilia. That is when I learned about the New Mexico Mounted Police and their historian, Chuck Hornung. His book, *The Thin Gray Line, The New Mexico Mounted Police* (published in 1971), was out of print, but I was fortunate enough to acquire a copy. I noticed on one of the back pages there was a drawing of the New Mexico State Police badge. Chuck had said that the mounted police was the "father" of the present-day state police. The book was fascinating, and I could not put it down. Chuck is a type of writer that holds the reader's attention and does not go on and on about historical data. He writes about real people, using the fruit of his 40 years of research.

Over the years, I made contact with Chuck and used his knowledge of the mounted police for future state police annuals. The story of these territorial rangers was fascinating. How many citizens and historians knew that there was a territory/statewide police force in the days when lawmen rode horses?

For 15 years, the New Mexico Mounted Police fought politicians and outlaws. They also had to fight corrupt and jealous county and local law enforcement officers. The county sheriffs were used to having their own way, until the rangers came on the scene, and collected revenue by bringing in the outlaws. The mounted police was a threat to county sheriffs, because the mounted police collected no rewards and did not stop at the county line. In the end, the mounted police department fell victim to politics more than anything else. There is no telling where the future would have taken this agency if not for the muddy politics of their era. Maybe I would have become a sergeant in the New Mexico Mounted Police instead of a sergeant in the New Mexico State Police.

Over the years, I have met with Chuck several times and enjoyed his collection of mounted police memorabilia. Those items and photographs brought the men to life. It seems strange to think that such hard and tough men were out there trailing the bad guys in the last days of New Mexico territory and the early days of statehood, and no one knew much about them until Chuck wrote his first book about these rangers.

In 2005, the centennial of the New Mexico Mounted Police, Chuck Hornung published *Fullerton's Rangers: A History of the New Mexico Territorial Mounted Police*. When I first saw the book, I wondered how anyone could fill 259 pages with interesting information about one year in the history of a frontier police organization, but Chuck did just that and made you what to learn more.

Chuck has now compiled this illustrated history of New Mexico's rangers. I wondered how it could get any better than his last two books. But it has. This is a book I could not put down. Chuck Hornung has done honor to the New Mexico Mounted Police with this visual account of their legendary history.

—Sgt. Ronald Taylor
New Mexico State Police Historian

ACKNOWLEDGMENTS

I have many people to thank for their help along the trail. Most of these people have, as individuals, been singled out in other works so as brothers and sisters of our large mounted police family let me say again, thank you. Special acknowledgment is given to my wife, our sons, and Ron and Pat Fuss. You have spent so many years encouraging and helping me to keep the promise and tell this story. The New Mexico Mounted Police Collection (NMMP) is a major repository for many of these images showcased in this book. Any image without a courtesy line is from my own personal collection.

PREFACE

I never intended to write an illustrated history of the New Mexico Mounted Police. In fact, I had never even heard of these lawmen of the last frontier in the southwest until I was a graduate student. Television and movie westerns had led the general public to understand that it was the Texas Rangers, with just a little help from the obscure Arizona Rangers, that brought law and order to the whole area "west of the Pecos" without any help from law enforcement officers in that mysterious void between Arizona and Texas called New Mexico.

I was attending school in Kentucky and my girlfriend, now my wife, was in school back east, so I spent long weekends in the university library. The 26 volumes of evidence for the Warren Commission Report made for frustrating reading material, as did the *New York Times*' coverage of the daily events of the Civil War. While looking through the 1911 edition of the *Encyclopedia Britannica*, I discovered a reference to the mounted police in an article about New Mexico. I loved the land of enchantment and had spent many summers working on a northeastern New Mexico ranch during my high school and college years.

During the rest of that term, I sought information about the mounted police from New Mexico's state archives and historical societies. I learned two things. First, little was known about the mounted police in their homeland, and secondly, two names seemed to come up when someone did know something about these rangers: Fred Fornoff and Fred Lambert. I was told that both men had died long ago. On a beautiful Sunday afternoon in June 1967, I came face-to-face with a living legend. I met Fred Lambert at his home in Cimarron. The story of that meeting is told in my book *Fullerton's Rangers*. It was that meeting that started my journey to record the adventures and to preserve the memory of *New Mexico's Rangers: The Mounted Police*.

This volume is possible only because for the past four decades we have slowly tracked the men of the mounted police, and along the way we have met many of their descendants and family friends. It has been a rewarding, sometimes tedious journey. When we took up the trail, few librarians or archivists had ever heard of the mounted police and so many others confused these horseback territorial state lawmen with a present-day volunteer group, the New Mexico Mounted Patrol, which assists the New Mexico State Police on special occasions. The New Mexico Mounted Police are the forefathers of the New Mexico State Police.

One

THE CLOSING FRONTIER

THE RISE OF MOUNTED POLICE

The Treaty of Guadalupe Hidalgo ended the war between the United States and the Mexican Republic in 1848. This treaty seeded Mexican lands that encompassed the present states of California, Arizona, New Mexico, and parts of southern Nevada and southern Colorado to the United States. The Territory of New Mexico was created from these lands by Congress as part of the Compromise of 1850.

The Gadsden Purchase Treaty established New Mexico's southern boundary with the Republic of Mexico in 1853 when Congress agreed to buy some disputed lands in the Mesilla Valley from Mexico for $10 million.

The boundary line between New Mexico and Arizona territories was authorized as the 32nd meridian in February 1863, but was not established on the ground until 1875. New Mexico's southern and eastern boundary with Texas was established in 1859, but a dispute with Texas over the eastern border was not settled until 1891, and the southern line argument continued until 1930. New Mexico's northern boundary line with Colorado was not finalized until 1960. This was 110 years after the territory had been established.

New Mexico Territory contained 121,666 square miles in a land mass extending 390 miles from north to south and 350 miles from east to west. Even today, New Mexico has less water per acre that any other state in the federal union.

At the turn of the 20th century, New Mexico Territory was the last refuge for bunko artists, rustlers, gamblers, and an assortment of other outlaw types. Members of the newly reorganized Texas Rangers and the infant Arizona Rangers had arrested, killed, or driven most of the shady characters out of their jurisdiction and into the Sunshine Territory, New Mexico's nickname before statehood. Colorado sheriffs and the Mexican federal police tightened the vice from the north and the south. New Mexico needed its own ranger force to combat the lawless element.

COUNCILMAN GRANVILLE ADDISON RICHARDSON. Granville Addison Richardson was an attorney and a Democrat. He saw the need for a New Mexico ranger force to deal with the territory's outlaw situation. As a councilman in 1899, he introduced a bill to create a 13-man company of territorial mounted police. The ranger force was designed to operate much like their namesake police force in Canada, thus the name. The force would cost the territory $9,120 per year for salaries. On a comparative scale, the captain was to be paid $200 per month, or slightly less than the average salary for a public school teacher. In later years, Richardson served in the 1910 New Mexico State Constitutional Convention, two terms in the New Mexico State Legislature, and ended his public career as judge of the fifth judicial district. A street in Roswell, his hometown, is named in his honor. (*History of New Mexico*, 1907.)

COUNCILMAN THOMAS D. BURNS. Thomas D. Burns, a Republican from Tierra Amarilla, was a banker, merchant, and stockraiser who represented Rio Arriba County and San Juan County in the council in 1899. Burns chaired the council's Territorial Affairs Committee, and on January 30, his committee was assigned to review Richardson's New Mexico Mounted Police Bill. The committee debated the need for a ranger force and the cost to taxpayers verses the desirability of the territory's stockgrower associations to bear the financial burden of the range riders. The council, on a split vote, sent the bill back to the committee to die. (*History of New Mexico*, 1907.)

GEORGE SCARBOROUGH. The Louisiana born George A. Scarborough was the leader of the Southwest New Mexico Cattle Protective Association's range detectives. They roamed across New Mexico's southern tier of counties seeking cattle rustlers in the late 1890s. Many supporters of a New Mexico ranger force saw Scarborough as the leading candidate to command a new ranger force. (John F. Fullerton.)

CHAMBER OF THE TERRITORIAL HOUSE OF REPRESENTATIVES. The leadership of the Republican-controlled 1899 Territorial House of Representatives supported the idea of a New Mexico ranger force to combat the growing menace to peace, safety, and economic development. The majority of the representatives, however, felt the livestock owners, who they believed would benefit most from a force of rangers, should pay the bill and not the taxpayers of the territory. (Museum of New Mexico.)

TERRITORIAL GOVERNOR MIGUEL ANTONIO OTERO JR. Miguel A. Otero became territorial governor in 1897. He privately supported a ranger force when the 33rd Legislative Assembly discussed the issue in 1899. Six years later, the governor publicly requested the territorial lawmakers to create a territorial police force. Council Bill 26, the mounted police legislation, provided that the governor was to be the commander in chief of the proposed territorial police, but a captain would serve as the day-to-day leader. (John F. Fullerton.)

FE NEW M[

HS | MR. GREER PROPOSES | LEGIS[
OLD | RELIEF FROM OUTLAWS | A

of the
Other

Mounted Police Force Urged As An Effectual Remedy for An Unfortunate State of Criminal Affairs in Southern New Mexico.

DSEA

a Coal
Play

Eleventh Da
Every memb
call, President
iain Shively le
al of the prev
approved.
The followin
Council Bill
providing for a
read twice and

THE *SANTA FE NEW MEXICAN*, JANUARY 26, 1905. In the six years since a territorial police force was first proposed in New Mexico, the criminal element had grown bolder, and their lawless actions were causing havoc with the territory's growing economy and the political push to achieve statehood. In 1901, the Texas State Legislature reorganized their ranger force and the Arizona Territory established a ranger service. Over the next few years, these rangers chased their problems into the Sunshine Territory. (*Santa Fe New Mexican* Archives.)

COUNCILMAN WILLIAM H. GREER. William Hugh Greer was a native of Iowa but spent his childhood in California. He became an attorney and married into a wealthy California family. He came to New Mexico Territory to manage his father-in-law's interest in the vast Victoria Land and Cattle Company. Greer served as point man for the livestock interest in the 36th Legislative Assembly and introduced the new plan for a ranger force. (*Albuquerque Morning Journal*, September 15, 1905.)

TERRITORIAL COUNCIL CHAMBER, 1905. On January 25, 1905, the 11th day of the 33rd New Mexico Legislative Assembly session, legislation to create a force of territorial police was introduced. Two weeks later, on February 9, following some modifications to the proposal in the Council Finance Committee, Amended Council Bill 26 was passed on a roll call vote and sent to the House of Representatives for that body's concurrent action. It passed, and the bill was signed into law. (Museum of New Mexico.)

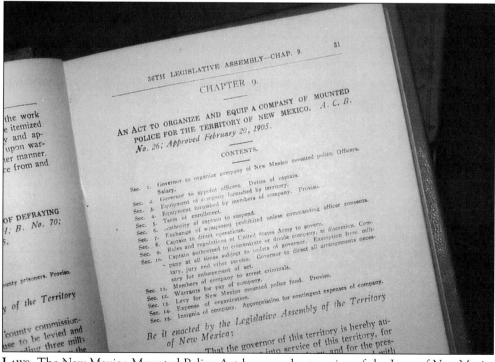

LAWS. The New Mexico Mounted Police Act became chapter nine of the *Laws of New Mexico 1905* when that year's laws were published. (NMMP.)

HON. SOLOMON LUNA. Solomon Luna, a native of Los Lunas, was a powerful influence within the Republican Party. As a national committee member, he was *jefe politico* and affectionately nicknamed "King Saul" by his many friends. Luna, a former Valencia County sheriff, was asked by Governor Otero to be part of the duo application screening committee to recommend the new ranger force. (*New Mexico Blue Book*, 1909.)

HON. HOLM O. BURSUM. Iowa born Holm O. Bursum came to New Mexico Territory as a teenager and made his mark on the livestock and mining industry. He was a distinguished former sheriff of Socorro County and superintendent of the territorial penitentiary. Bursum accepted Governor Otero's request to select the territory's new rangers with his usual zest for a new challenge. (*New Mexico Blue Book*, 1919.)

Two

FULLERTON'S RANGERS
1905–1906

The Mounted Police Act of 1905 mandated that the governor had 60 days to appoint the 11 members of the territorial police. Governor Otero named his friends Solomon Luna and Holm Bursum as a screening committee to recommend to him the best 11 men from the over 200 ranger applications the chief executive had received. The two men did their job, and on Friday, March 17, 1905, they gave their recommendations to the governor.

Governor Otero and John Fullerton, Socorro County assessor and rancher, met in Santa Fe for a late Saturday morning conference to discuss John's appointment as the captain of New Mexico's infant ranger service. Otero offered Fullerton the challenge, and later that afternoon, John took his oath of office as a territorial department head. The two men conferred again on Monday, Tuesday, and Wednesday, putting "meat on the bones" of the legislation that created the rangers.

On April Fool's Day 1905, ten days later, Captain Fullerton met with six of the eight men who would service as privates in the first company of mounted police. These men were gathered in Santa Fe in the governor's office to hear from Captain Fullerton on how he intended to operate the company. Lt. Cipriano Baca and Sgt. Robert W. Lewis, highly respected lawmen from Socorro County, were also present to take their oath of office.

Captain Fullerton gave his new rangers a couple of weeks to settle their business and family affairs before reporting to mounted police headquarters at Socorro. In mid-April, Lieutenant Baca and Sergeant Lewis led ranger patrols in search of rustlers and other types of "badmen" roaming the territory's vast, remote countryside.

Sam Ballard holds the dubious distinction of being the first man arrested by a New Mexico territorial ranger. Mounted policeman Will Dudley arrested Ballard for "larceny of stock" during a lonesome scout across the mountains of Lincoln County. The men of Fullerton's Rangers made 72 official arrests during their one year of operation.

JOHN FERGUSON FULLERTON. John Ferguson Fullerton was born in New Castle, Pennsylvania, in May 1856. When he was eight years old, his father moved the family to a farm in Scotland County, Missouri. A decade later, the Fullerton family moved south to St. Louis because Civil War service in the Union army had affected the senior Fullerton's health, and he needed a warmer and dryer climate. In the 1880s, a final move was made to Socorro County in New Mexico Territory. The Yankee blacksmith was going to try his hand at ranching on the southwestern plains at the base of the Rocky Mountains. (Irene Fullerton.)

John F. Fullerton and his Family. While living in St. Louis, Fullerton married a young woman from Louisiana named Susan Baker. The newlyweds joined the senior Fullertons on the San Augustin Plains in western Socorro County. Father and son started a sheep and cattle ranch and a trading post. John and Susan became parents to three sons. The oldest died at birth, and the third son and his mother died in a fever epidemic in 1893. This photograph was taken in Socorro during the fall of 1892. John Elmer, the middle son, is sitting on his father's lap. (Irene Fullerton.)

Capt. John F. Fullerton
new mexico Rangers

Capt. John F. Fullerton, NMMP. By the early 1900s, the Fullerton family had become prominent stockraisers. John's first and only attempt at elective office was to run as a Republican for Socorro County tax assessor in 1904. John won the election, but he served less than three months before Governor Otero appointed him the first captain of the mounted police on March 19, 1905. (Irene Fullerton.)

19

JOHN F. FULLERTON AS AN ELDERLY BUSINESSMAN. John F. Fullerton served as captain of the territorial police, popularly called Fullerton's Rangers, for just over a year. Herbert J. Hagerman, the man who replaced Miguel Otero as territorial governor, chose not to reappoint Fullerton as ranger captain. John felt that the new governor had deprived him the opportunity to complete his mission and receive credit for creating an effective territorial police. Fullerton sold his ranch, moved to Socorro, and spent the remainder of his life as an insurance agent. John died in January 1928 while visiting his sister and her family in San Diego, California. (Irene Fullerton.)

IRENE LAFONT FULLERTON AND DAUGHTER SUSAN FULLERTON LEVERETT. John Elmer Fullerton married Irene Grace LaFont and they had a long, adventuresome life together managing the family ranch and operating a Native American trading post. They had a daughter named Susan after John's mother, and she grew up to marry a World War II hero named William Leverett. Irene Fullerton was 105 years old when she died in 2002. This picture was taken in the front yard of the Leverett's Albuquerque home at the time of the author's first visit in 1984.

BIRD'S-EYE VIEW OF SOCORRO, NEW MEXICO. John F. Fullerton had watched Socorro grow from a small trading community to a thriving center of regional commerce for a vast underpopulated landmass. The city was the county seat for the largest county in the territory. The mounted police law required the captain to select "the most unprotected and exposed settlement of the territory" as his headquarters. The mounted police department was the only territorial agency not housed in Santa Fe. (NMMP.)

NEW MEXICO MOUNTED POLICE HEADQUARTERS AT SOCORRO. Captain Fullerton established his office in the Chambon Building on Court Street, a short walk to the Socorro County courthouse and jail. He paid Henry Chambon $9 per month for the space. Elfego Baca, the newly appointed district attorney, vacated his old law office and moved to the courthouse. Fullerton bought Baca's office furnishings for $51 and set up the territorial police's first headquarters. This picture was taken in 1968.

A LITTLE GAME ON THE OPEN RANGE

THE MOUNTED POLICE MISSION. The territorial police were established to protect New Mexico's vital livestock and mining interests, railroads, commerce, and citizens living in the remote sections of the territory from rustlers and other outlaw elements. The rangers were to assist local lawmen when possible, but if that was impossible for any reason, the mounted police's mission must come first in spite of protocol. The Mounted Police Act authorized the rangers to enforce federal and territorial laws, as well as local ordinances, anywhere within the territory. (Fred Lambert.)

LT. CIPRIANO BACA, NMMP. Cipriano Baca began his law enforcement career as an undercover stock association detective and later worked as a Grant County deputy sheriff at Deming, a Socorro County deputy sheriff at Mogollon, and a deputy U.S. marshal. Cipriano was elected Socorro County tax assessor in November 1896. Next, Cipriano Baca worked with his old friend Holm Bursum at the territorial prison in Santa Fe. Gov. Miguel Otero named Baca the first sheriff of the newly created Luna County in the spring of 1901. (Cipriana Baca Randolph.)

CIPRIANA BACA (RANDOLPH)
DATE UNKNOWN

CIPRIANA BACA RANDOLPH. Cipriana Baca Randolph was born on January 28, 1902, in Deming, Luna County, New Mexico Territory. The author first made contact with Cipriana in 1982 and continued a friendship over the next quarter century as she helped the author do research for a biography on her father. Cipriana Baca Randolph died in Whittier, California, in June 1998. (Cipriana Baca Randolph.)

CIPRIANO BACA AND HIS GRANDCHILDREN. Cipriano Baca's daughters, Maisie Baca Amos and Cipriana Baca Randolph, brought their children to visit their grandfather at his north Albuquerque home in September 1935. Maisie Amos was a young widow with young kids and Cipriana's daughter was just a couple of years old. Baca died a year later and was buried about a half a mile from his home. The young boy in the picture is John Amos. Over a half-century later, he placed a lovely marker over his grandfather's grave. (John Amos.)

CIPRIANA BACA RANDOLPH AND FRIEND, 1984. Cipriana Baca Randolph and Irene Grace LaFont Fullerton were friends in old age. Cipriana met Irene while she attended the Albuquerque Business College. Cipriana's aunt and ward, Effie Berry Stauder, and Irene were friends from their high school days in Socorro. The two aging ladies said goodbye for the last time in June 1984 at the Albuquerque SunPort just before Cipriana, who had been visiting in Socorro, boarded a return flight to her West Coast home.

MOUNTED POLICE BRING A PRISONER TO JUSTICE.
During June, July, and August 1905, Lt. Cipriano
Baca led rangers Julius Meyer and Octaviano Perea
on a hunt for the rustling Magnum brothers. This
photograph was taken with Lieutenant Baca's
Kodak camera and depicts one of the brothers,
in handcuffs, being brought to face justice.
Lieutenant Baca is riding beside the prisoner
as rangers Perea and Meyer ride escort. The
prisoner was taken to jail at Aztec and placed
in the San Juan County jail. (Fred Lambert.)

SGT. ROBERT W. "STUTTERING BOB" LEWIS.
Robert W. Lewis was 19 years old when he rode
with a cattle drive to New Mexico Territory. His
speech impediment did not stop the 6-foot, 2-inch
youth from being the life of any party. He loved
watermelon and was a top-tier practical joker. He
began his law enforcement career in 1902 when
the newly elected Socorro County sheriff, Leandro
Baca, asked Lewis to accept the post of deputy
sheriff and jailer. This photograph was taken in
1935 when Lewis was the marshal at Magdalena.
(*New Mexico Magazine*, October 1935.)

THE WINTER-LONG HUNT. Howard Chenoworth was sentenced to 50 years in the territorial prison in August 1904 for killing two Silver City lawmen and wounding another man. He escaped jail and headed for Old Mexico during the coldest winter in seven years. Sergeant Lewis spent 71 days on the hunt. During his absence, his daughter, Una, was badly burned in a trash fire and died. No one knew the location of the ranger sergeant, and newspapers reported that outlaws had killed him. (*Santa Fe New Mexican* Archives.)

BOB LEWIS AS AN OLD WARRIOR. This 1949 picture shows Bob Lewis sitting in his overstuffed chair at his Magdalena home. Bob has his hat in his lap and a shoulder holster under his left arm holding a Colt .38 caliber pistol. Lewis left the mounted police after four years and returned to the cattle business before returning to law enforcement as marshal at Magdalena. In the closing days of the Great Depression, Lewis directed a Civilian Conservation Corps camp near Albuquerque. Rheumatism finely did what outlaws could not; Lewis gave up the active life at 73. (Howard Bryan.)

GEORGE ELKINS, RANGER NO. 1.
George M. Elkins was first, last, and
always a cowman. He was fearless
on the hunt and a loving father and
husband at home. For years before
and after his service to the territory,
George Elkins, standing in this
1913 photograph, was the foreman
of the vast Hatchet Ranch in the
rugged mountains of New Mexico's
Bootheel. He was also a livestock
inspector and was assassinated in
old Mexico in June 1926 by border
rustlers. (Chandler Elkins.)

JULIUS MEYER, RANGER NO. 2. The
author had the pleasure of meeting
and corresponding with three of
Julius Meyer's many grandchildren.
He had three wives. Meyer was born
near Paris, Missouri, in July 1866. He
spoke excellent Spanish and enjoyed
the native culture. Meyer was a
Torrance County deputy sheriff, living
at Estancia, when he was selected
as a territorial ranger in March
1905. He served four years with the
mounted police. (Mrs. I. B. Singer.)

JULIUS MEYER IN OLD AGE. Julius Meyer was elected sheriff of Torrance County in November 1908 and served in the office for the next decade. He also operated an auto repair shop in Estancia and a small ranch and farm near Willard. Meyer was a partner along with Captain Fornoff and Earl Scott in a salt supply company, operating a digging operation at a salt lake in Torrance County. Failing heath sent Julius to California with an advanced case of consumption in the late 1930s. (Steve Meyer.)

WILLIAM E. DUDLEY, RANGER NO. 4. William E. Dudley hailed from Tyler, Texas. He spoke fluent Spanish and became a noted classical orator and private school headmaster. His wife, Josie, was also an excellent educator and earned an Alamogordo school named in her honor. Will's actions in the field earned the former headmaster high regard and professional respect as a territorial peace officer. This picture shows Will Dudley mounted on his horse, Keno, smoking a cigar and wearing the mounted police badge on his jacket. (Frank Shofner.)

OCTAVIANO PEREA, RANGER NO. 5. Octaviano Perea was a native New Mexican schoolteacher and Spanish translator, court interpreter, and notary public who loved to play cards and race horses. When his father was elected sheriff of Lincoln County, Octaviano became chief deputy and jailor. In 1904, Perea moved his family to Alamogordo and published a Spanish-language newspaper. Perea resigned from the rangers after a few months and moved to Old Mexico. Years later, he returned to Lincoln County. (Lincoln County Historical Society.)

A MOUNTAIN SCOUT. Fullerton's Rangers were in constant motion. They seemed to always be coming from or going on scout duty in the mountains or over the vast range country, seeking rustlers. This photograph is part of the mounted police collection assembled by Fred Lambert. The ranger leading the sting of packhorses is thought to be Octaviano Perea, who was on a long scout with Julius Meyer and Lieutenant Baca in the summer of 1905. Baca had a camera on that three-month trip. (Fred Lambert.)

HERB MCGRATH, RANGER NO. 6. Herbert James McGrath was highly respected and well liked while he, center in the photograph, quarterbacked the 1893 football team at what today is New Mexico State University. McGrath was a Grant County deputy sheriff when he killed the men who held up a saloon in his area. Herb served only nine months with Fullerton's Rangers. He resigned claiming he could make more money serving local warrants and collecting fines and reward money then his ranger salary paid. (*New Mexico Collegian*, 1893.)

JESSIE LAFETTIE "L. F." AVANT, RANGER NO. 7. Jesse LaFettie Avant, called Fate by family and close friends, was born on the family ranch in Texas and grew up to be a 6-foot, 2-inch, 170-pound, blue-eyed, sandy red-haired lifetime rancher. He married Ella Mae Simonds on her family's homestead near Chadbourne. The young couple settled on their own homestead near Cotulla, 65 miles north of the Rio Grande in rustler country. Avant joined the Texas Rangers to help end the outlaw problem. (Jettie Avant Sullenger.)

Fate Avant Branding Cattle on his Ranch. A prolonged drought caused Avant to lose his Texas homestead in the mid-1890s. He traveled to eastern New Mexico as a sowing machine salesman before taking up a 3,800-acre farm ranch homestead near Capitan. He served five years with New Mexico's rangers. Avant sold his Lincoln County property in 1915 and settled in Sierra County. A 1920 drought caused Avant to lose his ranch, and he spent the rest of his days working as a cattle inspector and a day laborer. (Jettie Avant Sullenger.)

Welch and Titsworth Store in Capitan, 1905. The site of Capitan on the Salado Flat was first homesteaded in 1884. George A. Titsworth came to Capitan to make his fortune and bought a half interest in E. B. Welch's store in the winter of 1901. He soon bought out his senior partner. Titsworth was a man of small stature and a pleasant nature. He was, however, a very cunning businessman; some said he was ruthless. The Titsworth Store was remodeled and enlarged several times before it was torn down to make room for a small strip mall. (Capitan Museum.)

INTERIOR OF THE WELCH AND TITSWORTH STORE AT CAPITAN, 1905. George Titsworth operated his mercantile store with separate departments for shopper convenience. It was also a way for Titsworth to maintain tight inventory controls and to help determine customer needs and wants. He offered a liberal charge account policy, but it came with a substantial interest rate and stringent payment deadlines. Over the years, Titsworth accumulated vast landholdings by accepting the property of native New Mexicans as payment for their indebtedness at his store. (Capitan Museum.)

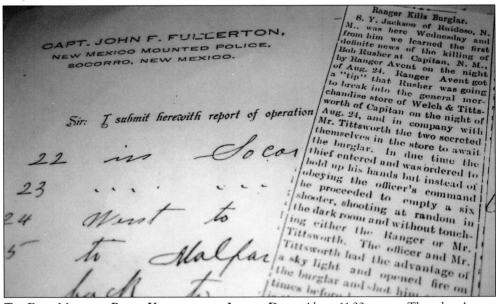

THE FIRST MOUNTED POLICE KILLING IN THE LINE OF DUTY. About 11:20 p.m. on Thursday, August 24, 1905, Ranger Fate Avant and George Titsworth were concealed in the mercantile. The ranger had been tipped that someone might try to rob the store. When Avant ordered Robert Rusher to surrender, the career criminal emptied his .38-caliber automatic pistol before the ranger blasted him with his shotgun. Early the next morning, a coroner's jury found that "the deceased met his death while resisting lawful arrest." (NMMP.)

TERRITORIAL ATTORNEY GENERAL GEORGE W. PRICHARD. Territorial attorney general George W. Prichard issued Opinion No. 252 on May 19, 1905, stating that a territorial policeman "may use sufficient force, in making arrests, where resisted, to effect his purpose." Fate Avant's lethal action eliminated any doubt that the rangers of the new mounted police force would give no quarter in arresting suspected criminals. (*History of New Mexico*, 1907.)

FULLERTON'S RANGERS ASSEMBLED FOR THE TERRITORIAL FAIR PARADE, 1905. The Territorial Fair Committee requested that the mounted police lead the annual fair parade in 1905. The rangers gathered at the home of U.S. Marshal Creighton M. Foraker near Old Town Albuquerque for a staging area. This photograph was in Fred Lambert's mounted police collection and identified as the rangers gathered at Foraker's ranch. (Fred Lambert.)

NATIONAL FLAG CARRIED BY THE MOUNTED POLICE. The 25th annual New Mexico Territorial Fair at Albuquerque and the Northern New Mexico Fair at East Las Vegas were held in the fall of 1905 and were the only times that Fullerton's Rangers were ever assembled at the same place. Captain Fullerton rode at the head of the two columns of grey-clad mounted police led by Lt. Cipriano Baca and Sgt. Robert Lewis. The rangers carried a 45-star national flag and an insignia for the mounted police. (NMMP.)

Three

CAP FORNOFF'S BOYS
1906–1913

The new territorial governor asked John Fullerton to resign as captain of the territorial police, effective April 1906. The next day, Gov. H. J. Hagerman named Deputy U.S. Marshal Fred Fornoff as the new leader of the rangers. Fornoff met with his command on April 2 and outlined the new operation. He asked the rangers to reenlist and continue their good work. The most drastic change was moving the headquarters to the capitol in Santa Fe, discontinuing the gray ranger uniform, and issuing a new star-shaped badge.

The 1911 edition of the *Encyclopedia Britannica* contained a short account of the New Mexico Mounted Police:

> "A rather unusual institution within New Mexico is the Mounted Police, who numbered 11 (men) in 1907, whose work was almost entirely in the cattle country, and who had authority to patrol the entire Territory and make arrests or to preserve order wherever their presence was needed, unhampered by the restrictions limiting the jurisdiction of local police."

This reorganized second company of New Mexico Mounted Police soon earned the nickname of Fornoff's Boys. They earned the honor daily for almost eight years and carried the memory of working in the mountie service with them for the rest of their lives.

TERRITORIAL GOVERNOR HERBERT J. HAGERMAN. The Cornell University educated Herbert James Hagerman was a man of stern moral character. He believed that Pres. Theodore Roosevelt had anointed him as the "White Knight" savior of New Mexico, sent to clean up the "corrupt political machine" governing the territory. In truth, Roosevelt wanted Arizona and New Mexico to join the union as one state and Governor Otero opposed the idea, so he was not reappointed as chief executive. When the president did not get his joint statehood wish delivered by Hagerman, he was requested to resign in late April 1907. Captain Fullerton and Wisconsin native Hagerman clashed from the start and the governor fired him. (Fred Fornoff.)

ACTING TERRITORIAL GOVERNOR J. WALLACE RAYNOLDS. James Wallace Raynolds was appointed secretary of New Mexico Territory in 1901. During the years that Raynolds served as secretary, he acted as governor whenever the chief executive was absent from the territory on vacation or official business. The longest period he acted as governor was during the summer of 1907. Raynolds supported the mounted police. He was named superintendent of the territorial penitentiary in April 1909 and held that post until failing health ended his life in March 1910. (Miguel A. Otero Papers.)

TERRITORIAL GOVERNOR GEORGE CURRY. A native of Bayou Sara, Louisiana, Curry came to New Mexico in 1879 and entered the political arena. He served as probate clerk, county tax assessor, sheriff, and legislative councilman. In 1898, he was a captain of Roosevelt's Rough Riders in the war with Spain and also fought in the Philippine Insurrection. President Roosevelt named Curry governor of New Mexico in 1907. Curry and Captain Fornoff were good friends and worked well together. (Museum of New Mexico.)

TERRITORIAL GOVERNOR WILLIAM J. MILLS. Born in Mississippi in 1849, William Joseph Mills graduated from the Yale University law school and served in both houses of the Connecticut legislature before coming to New Mexico to open a law office. Pres. William McKinley appointed him chief justice of the New Mexico Territorial Supreme Court in 1898, and Mills served that office until Pres. William H. Taft named him the last territorial governor in 1910. Mills died on Christmas Eve 1915 at his home in East Las Vegas, New Mexico. (Museum of New Mexico.)

NMMP HEADQUARTERS AT THE CAPITOL IN SANTA FE. The building was called the "new capitol" after it was completed in 1900. It was constructed to replace the former capitol that had burned from an arsonist's fire. The structure was designed after the national capitol in Washington, D.C., and continued to be used until 1966. The building was enlarged and remodeled to resemble a large adobe structure, and the dome removed. The building is now used by a government agency. (Museum of New Mexico.)

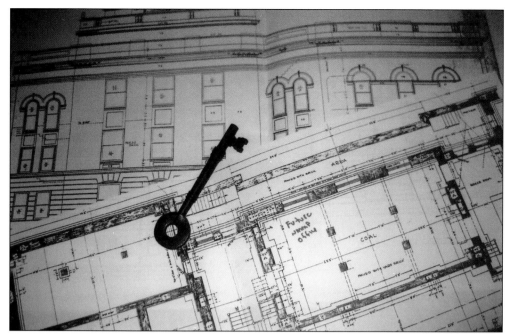

THE MOUNTED POLICE OFFICE. This photograph shows the 1900 blueprints of the section of the capitol where the mounted police office was located from 1906 to 1913. The two-room suite was on the first floor, near the south entrance, and contained secondhand furnishing from other government departments. Fred Lambert acquired the brass key to the mounted police office in December 1913 when the office was remodeled and turned into a meeting room for use by a house legislative committee. (New Mexico State Record Center and Archives.)

DESK FLAG. This small 48-star desk flag, made of heavy silk, belonged to Gus Koch, a nephew of a wealthy St. Louis businessman and political leader, who served as the mounted police office clerk during the first years of the state government. The flag sat on a file cabinet in the clerk's room in the two-room mounted police headquarters in the capitol. Koch gave Fred Lambert the flag as a remembrance of their days in the mounted police. (Fred Lambert.)

FRED FORNOFF AT DENVER, 1905. This picture was taken outside the U.S. Mint in Denver in 1905. Fred Fornoff was then a Secret Service agent assigned by the Treasury Department to hunt down counterfeiters operating in the Rocky Mountain west. Fornoff soon returned to New Mexico and resumed his duties as a federal deputy marshal in Albuquerque. (Fred Fornoff Jr.)

CAPT. FRED FORNOFF, 1906–1913. Frederic Fornoff was born in Baltimore, Maryland, in February 1859 and followed his big brother west in the early 1880s. In November 1894, Albuquerque's mayor appointed Fred as the town marshal, and he held the office until June 1897 when a new mayor named another man as the marshal. Fornoff was reappointed Albuquerque marshal in April 1898 but only served briefly before he joined New Mexico's company of Rough Riders to fight the Spanish in Cuba. (Fred Fornoff Jr.)

CAPTAIN FORNOFF'S NMMP POCKET COMMISSION. Fred Fornoff served as captain of the New Mexico Mounted Police from April 2, 1906, until November 30, 1913. Captain Fornoff was a man of commanding appearance, and his deep voice sounded authoritative. In detective work, Fornoff was a disciple of Sherlock Holmes; he believed in working slowly. One of his favorite remarks was "give it time," but he never lost time in getting into action when the "time" arrived. (Fred Fornoff Jr.)

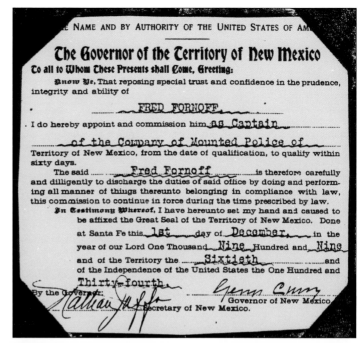

NAME AND BY AUTHORITY OF THE UNITED STATES OF AM

The Governor of the Territory of New Mexico

To all to Whom These Presents shall Come, Greeting:

Know Ye, That reposing special trust and confidence in the prudence, integrity and ability of

FRED FORNOFF

I do hereby appoint and commission him as Captain of the Company of Mounted Police of Territory of New Mexico, from the date of qualification, to qualify within sixty days.

The said Fred Fornoff is therefore carefully and diligently to discharge the duties of said office by doing and performing all manner of things thereunto belonging in compliance with law, this commission to continue in force during the time prescribed by law.

In Testimony Whereof, I have hereunto set my hand and caused to be affixed the Great Seal of the Territory of New Mexico. Done at Santa Fe this 1st day of December, in the year of our Lord One Thousand Nine Hundred and Nine and of the Territory the Sixtieth and of the Independence of the United States the One Hundred and Thirty-fourth.

By the Governor:

Secretary of New Mexico.

Governor of New Mexico.

CAPTAIN FORNOFF'S MINIATURE NMMP BADGES. Captain Fornoff was a classic dapper dresser of his era. He wore a business suit when on duty and favored the color brown. The captain had two miniature silver mounted police stars designed by a Santa Fe jeweler for his personal use. One was a lapel pin he worn instead of the regular issue badge his men wore when on duty. The second star was worn as a watch fob when he chose not to draw attention to himself when he was working in the field. (George Virgines.)

FRED FORNOFF'S MEMORIES. This photograph shows Fred Fornoff's custom-engraved, silver Albuquerque city marshal's badge, the Bernalillo County deputy sheriff's badge he wore in the 1920s, and a beaded NMMP leather ribbon presented to him as a gift in 1912 in celebration of New Mexico's statehood. (Fred Fornoff Jr.)

FRED FORNOFF JR. WITH HIS FATHER'S WINCHESTER. This picture was taken in the family room of Lois and Fred Fornoff Jr.'s north Albuquerque home in the summer of 1991. The author and his wife had a very pleasant visit with the Fornoff's that afternoon. Fred is holding his father's .44-40 Winchester. Captain Fornoff liked a heavy weapon, so he carried this long rifle when he made field trips as a deputy U.S. marshal and later as captain of the mounted police. (NMMP.)

CAPTAIN FORNOFF, LIEUTENANT BACA, AND U.S. MARSHAL FORAKER. Grant County rancher Creighton M. Foraker was appointed as the U.S. marshal for New Mexico Territory by Pres. William McKinley in early 1897 and served until statehood was granted in January 1912. In 1904, Foraker posed for a photograph with five of his field deputies (only two are shown above). Fornoff is seated to the right of Foraker, and Cipriano Baca is leaning on Fornoff's chair. These three Republican lawmen were friends and worked well together. (Mary Foraker.)

LT. CIPRIANO BACA. Baca resigned from the mounted police in January 1907. At the time, he was very popular among the rangers and the general public. His arrest and conviction rate made him the most efficient member of the early territorial police. Baca worked as a railroad detective, town marshal of Dawson, and deputy sheriff and constable at Mogollon before returning to the reorganized state rangers in 1918. (NMMP.)

Lt. John Collier. John Wesley Collier was born into a Texas ranching family in 1871. In the 1890s, Collier drove a hack (cab) in El Paso before moving on to Silver City, New Mexico, and being hired as a deputy sheriff. Collier was first appointed to the mounted police in May 1906. He served as a ranger or deputy U.S. marshal until the spring of 1913. John later became a railroad special agent. He died in Wichita, Kansas, in 1964. (Coral Collier Horton.)

CORAL COLLIER HORTON AND CHUCK HORNUNG. Coral Collier Horton was the one child of John and Louise Rose Menkemeyer Collier that lived to adulthood. She was born in Estancia, New Mexico, in January 1911. This picture was taken on the author's visit to Horton's Tucson home shortly after her 95th birthday. She was a very nice lady and had a deep love and respect for her father.

GEORGE FRED MURRAY, NMMP. Fred Murray was a rugged outdoorsman who was born in Dallas, Texas, in March 1877. Murray took on the corrupt political machine in McKinley County and arrested one of the leaders who served as a justice of the peace. The McKinley County sheriff arrested Murray on charges of bootlegging and manslaughter. Murray went to prison, and the justice of the peace was elected to the legislature. The governor pardoned the former ranger, and he continued his fight for justice. (New Mexico State Records Center and Archives.)

SGT. WILL DUDLEY. When Sgt. Bob Lewis was promoted to lieutenant in March 1908, Captain Fornoff requested the governor to name Dudley to the sergeant's post. In early October 1910, Will Dudley resigned from the rangers and became the marshal of Dawson in Colfax County. Will was a Democrat and a Methodist-South member, who in the late 1910s served as a Baptist minister in Kansas, quoting the Bible and Shakespeare with equal force. (Frank Shofner.)

WILL DUDLEY'S THINGS. Will Dudley held a commission as a lieutenant in the New Mexico National Guard and won numerous local and national marksmanship competitions. One of these shooting medals is pictured here along with a hunting knife that Dudley made from a deer he killed in the Sacramento Mountains in 1908. The small lapel pin flag was a security detail identification used at the Republican Territorial Convention in 1908. (Frank Shofner.)

PAGE B. OTERO, NMMP OFFICE CLERK. Page Blackwell Otero was a deputy U.S. marshal and clerk of the U.S. Land Commissioner's Office before being appointed New Mexico's first territorial game warden in 1903. Otero was the mounted police office clerk from April 1908 until September 1910 when the position was abolished. He compiled the Fornoff Report, information developed by the mounted police's investigation into the murder of Pat Garrett in 1909. Otero died in California on the verge of poverty in the 1930s. (New Mexico Department of Game and Fish.)

Capt. Fred Fornoff considered William "Billy the Kid" Bonney a viper and a danger to society. He often said, "No history book ought to have a picture of that little murderer." Fornoff held only slightly more respect for Pat Garrett, the man who killed the young outlaw. When the former Dona Ana County sheriff was killed in 1908, Governor Curry asked Fornoff to investigate the circumstances of Garrett's death. With the help of Cipriano Baca, Fornoff developed information that established a conspiracy to legally steal Pat Garrett's ranch property for use by a Chinese smuggling ring as an area to secret their contraband. The mounted police's evidence was compiled by the rangers' office clerk into a dossier that Fornoff gave to the governor for prosecution by the attorney general; this investigation summation is called "The Fornoff Report." None of the mounted police's information was used at the trial of the confessed killer of Pat Garrett. The Fornoff Report has disappeared from the official records. (Garrett's badge courtesy of the Ruidoso River Museum.)

BEAL FAMILY. This photograph was taken in the front yard of the Beal residence in Deming, New Mexico. The woman standing on the left is John's wife, Julia Wyatt Beal. Julia and John separated after the children were grown. Shortly before her death, Julia told her life story, and it was tape-recorded. In this narration, Julia describes her husband as a wife beater and a dictator to his children. The author knew three of the Beal children, and only one of them had a kind word about their father; she was also the only one who had his picture. (Olive Beal-Posey.)

SGT. JOHN A. BEAL. John Alexander Beal was born in Arkansas in the fall of 1865, but grew up on a ranch-farm in Texas. He worked for the El Paso and Southwestern Railroad as a section foreman before becoming a deputy sheriff at Luna County. Beal had a quick temper and a hard right fist. He was a southern Democrat when appointed to the mounted police in November 1907. He had shot a man earlier that summer. When he worked as a New Mexico Ranger, John carried a Colt .30-30 automatic pistol in a right hip spring holster. He was a dead shot. (Olive Beal-Posey.)

BIRD'S-EYE VIEW OF MOGOLLON, NEW MEXICO. The author and Jim Stauder, a relative of Cipriano Baca on his wife Mary Berry's side of the marriage, made an exploratory expedition in 2008 to the ghost town of Mogollon. The author climbed to the same mountaintop ledge that the 1895 photographer used in this picture. Cipriano Baca's meat market is visible on the left side of the road near the center of the town. It was a beautiful spring day. (Jim Stauder.)

SHOOT-OUT AT MOGOLLON, 1910. A series of stage robberies caused Captain Fornoff to sent John Beal to Mogollon to investigate the robberies. Local business leaders, including deputy sheriff Charley Clark and the justice of the peace, were implicated in questionable enterprises. Both the justice of the peace and the deputy were removed from office due to Beal's investigation. The displaced deputy decided to remove Beal with a bullet, but when he sprung his ambush, his shot missed. Beal's return fire did not. (*Albuquerque Journal* Archives.)

ALBUQUERQU

THIRTY-SECOND YEAR. Vol. CXXVII, No. 63.　　　ALBUQUERQ

MOUNTED POLICE FIRED ONLY IN SELF DEFENSE DECLARES CAPTAIN FRED FORNOFF

SALOON KEEPER CLARK SLAIN IN DELIBERATE PLOT TO KILL THE RANGERS, IS CHIEF'S STORY

Beal in and we took a drink, went to the back of the house handed him the warrant. He me no s— of a b— of a sheriff arrest him and then told me t ahead of him and he got his first. Craig Williams was p and I deputized him to help m rest Beal. Bea' had a gun i hand. I didn't; I had my gun i pants. I said to Craig, "I don't that I have a right to hurt hir didn't aim to disarm him. Aft stepped out of the door he beg shoot. After the first shots i wrist and shoulder I stepped when he shot again. I was sta by the door leading into the b shop. I walked into the barber to get in the dark, and then sat on a chair."

FUNERAL OF CLARK WILL
BE LARGELY ATTEN
[Special Correspondence to Morning Jo
Mogollon, N. M., Aug.
Mounted Policemen Beal and Pu
charged with the shooting of Sa
keeper Charles Clark here, rode
Mogollon this evening in charg
Sheriff Sanchez and Sergeant C
of the mounted police, the whole
alcade being fully armed. Bea
Putnam, it is said, took refuge i

CHARLEY CLARK GRAVE SITE. Charles Clark died from his wound on August 28, 1910, and was buried on the other side of the mountain from Mogollon at the smaller mining camp of Cooney. Clark was buried in the Cooney Cemetery along Mineral Creek in Cooney Canyon just behind the hug rock marking Cooney's grave; Native Americans killed the prospector in the 1880s. Clark was a month short of his 42nd birthday when he died. He left a wife and some small children.

SOCORRO COUNTY COURTHOUSE. The chamber of the district court in the Socorro County Courthouse was the scene of the mounted police murder trial. The saloon element in Mogollon had employed top lawyers to help prosecute the case, but the 12-man jury found the rangers justified in the performance of their duty. The cause of law and order had won a victory, and the reputation of the mounted police not to back down in the face of danger, death, or powerful moneyed influence was sustained. (Jim Stauder.)

JAMES ALEXANDER "ALEX" STREET. James Alexander Street was born near Ripley, Mississippi, and became a true frontier adventurer and entrepreneur. He spent his youth in the Indian Territory before coming to New Mexico to work for the Bell Ranch. (Eula Street Sands.)

ALEX STREET. Street was one of the founders of the tent settlement known as Six-Shooter Siding along the right-of-way for the Chicago, Rock Island, and Pacific Railroad. In 1901, the name was changed to Douglas, but the growing community soon became known as Tucumcari, named after a nearby mountain. The Territorial Legislative Assembly created Quay County and made Tucumcari the county seat in 1903. Street was appointed the county's first sheriff and was elected to that office as a Democrat for 12 years. He also became Tucumcari's mayor in 1908. Street operated a livery stable in Tucumcari. On November 3, 1910, Alex Street was appointed to the mounted police and served until the end of November 1913. This picture shows Alex Street riding his favorite mare, Ida Reed, around 1910. (Courtesy of Jewel Street Pickerel.)

ALEX STREET'S FUNERAL ESCORT, 1937. Alex Street joined the Department of Justice's Bureau of Investigation in 1922, serving 15 years with the "G-Men" and earning the reputation as one of their best field agents. When Street retired from the FBI in May 1937, Governor Tingley hired him as a special investigator for the infant New Mexico State Police. He died in August 1937 in Albuquerque, and the state police escorted his body to Tucumcari. This picture was taken as the escort came into town headed for the Baptist church for Street's funeral. (Sgt. Ron Taylor, NMSP.)

BOONE VAUGHN. Boone Chatman Vaughn was born in Fosterburg, Illinois, in April 1861 and died in San Juan County, New Mexico, in January 1937. Vaughn was a horse rancher near Farmington. He ran as a Democrat and was elected and reelected sheriff, thus becoming the first person to serve two consecutive terms as San Juan County sheriff. Vaughn was appointed a mounted police on November 2, 1909, and served for 29 days before the rangers were downsized, and he lost his job. (San Juan County Sheriff's Department.)

FRED HIGGINS. Fred Higgins led an adventuresome life on the Arizona and New Mexico frontier. In the 1890s, he earned a killer reputation as a deputy U.S. marshal in a half a dozen fights that ended some outlaw's career. Higgins settled in Roswell, New Mexico, as town marshal until he was elected, as a Democrat, sheriff of Chaves County in 1898. He served in that office until the end of 1905. In September 1907, Higgins pinned on a territorial ranger star. He killed one man in a railroad station altercation in March 1909 and another man in a jail fight in Las Cruces in March 1911. (Chaves County Sheriff's Department.)

LEANDRO BACA. Leandro Baca served four years as assessor of Socorro County before becoming a lawman. He was elected sheriff in 1902 and reelected in 1904. Baca was appointed as a mounted police in March 1908 and served as a territorial officer until Captain Fornoff requested his resignation in October 1909 for excessive public use of liquor. In 1919, Governor Larrazolo appointed Baca to the reorganized mounted police led by Capt. A. A. Sena. Leandro was appointed the first sheriff of Catron County in 1921. (*History of New Mexico: Its Resources and People,* 1907.)

MILES CICERO STEWART. Miles Cicero Stewart served for 11 years as the sheriff of Eddy County, New Mexico. The Democrat was first appointed to the office in 1897 and then won his next five elections. During his time out of the sheriff's office, Governor Curry appointed Stewart to the mounted police, and he served nine months until he again assumed the sheriff's office. He then served as Eddy County's chief lawman for the next eight years. Stewart made five arrests as a territorial ranger. (Howard Bryan.)

ROBERT "BOB" BURCH. Robert Burch was born in Tennessee and came to New Mexico to make his fortune in the livestock business. One contemporary said that Burch did "nervy work" when he was hunting rustlers. He worked as a Dona Ana County lawman for many years and served as a territorial ranger from May 1906 to September 1907. Burch is shown at the left of another Las Cruces officer named Morgan Llewellyn. (New Mexico State University Library and Special Collections.)

ROBERT FRANK VANCE. Frank Vance, former marshal at Dawson and former New Mexico Mounted Police, was murdered in Cokedale, Colorado, in January 1912 by the coal camp's marshal. Vance only served five months with the rangers in mid-1907, but his death caused shock waves in the ranger force. Vance had been investigating the 1908 payroll robbery from the French railroad station. His friend Fred Lambert investigated Vance's killing and was almost killed for his trouble. The Colorado authorities refused to act on the evidence Lambert collected, and the men who killed Vance were never prosecuted. (Fred Lambert.)

FRED LAMBERT IN AUGUST 1911. Fred Lambert was born on January 23, 1887 in Cimarron, New Mexico. As a teenager, he worked in the family's large hotel and saloon complex, plus a small cattle ranch near town. Lambert served as Cimarron precinct constable, deputy sheriff, deputy territorial game warden, and Cimarron's first town marshal all before his 23rd birthday. In August 1911, Lambert was appointed by Governor Mills as the youngest man ever named to the territorial police. Captain Fornoff affectionately referred to Lambert as the "Kid." This picture was taken in Cimarron on August 12, 1911, on the occasion of Lambert taking his oath of office as a territorial ranger. He is wearing his star. (Fred Lambert.)

FRED LAMBERT'S RIDING GAUNTLETS. These are the riding gloves that Fred Lambert wore during his years as a mounted police officer. (Fred Lambert.)

FRED LAMBERT ON SCOUT DUTY. This photograph was taken in the fall of 1911 as Fred Lambert was returning to Cimarron from an extended rustler hunt in the mountains of Colfax County. Note the extra large bedroll tied behind Lambert's saddle and the lumberjack-style cap that he is wearing to keep his ears warm. (Fred Lambert.)

ANDREAS CALLES, PRISONER NO. 1454. Andreas Calles holds the dubious honor of being the only outlaw to have been arrested by three different mounted police for three different crimes. Fred Lambert arrested him for the last time, and Calles served a long sentence in the penitentiary. (New Mexico State Records Center and Archives.)

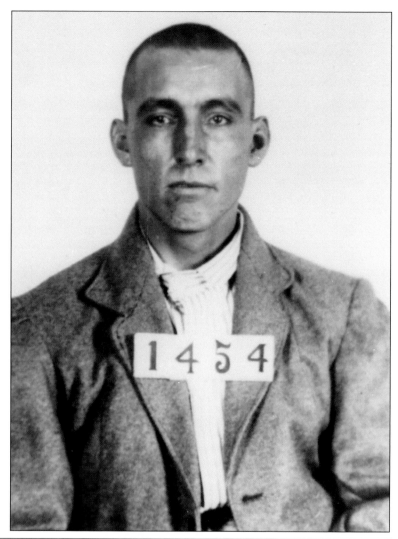

FRED FORNOFF, Captain

P. O. BOX 451

STATE OF NEW MEXICO
HEADQUARTERS OF MOUNTED POLICE
SANTA FE, NEW MEXICO

STATE MOUNTED POLICE LETTERHEAD. The State of New Mexico was born on Saturday, January 6, 1912, when Pres. William H. Taft signed the legislation admitting the territory into the union as the 47th state. The new state government took office on Monday, January 15, and with that move, all the functions of the state were in force, including the six-man state police. The new stationery conveyed the authority of the mounted police to protect the citizens of the "Sunshine State." This stationery was used until the state police agency was disbanded on December 1, 1913. (Fred Lambert.)

A Self-Portrait of Fred Lambert. This is a self-portrait of Fred Lambert done in pen and ink for a book of poetic tales written and illustrated by Lambert. First published in the late 1940s, *Bygone Days of the Old West* was republished in 1970 shortly before Lambert's death. The drawing plainly shows Lambert's gun belt, gloves, first aid kit, saddle carbine, ranger star, spurs, and horse bridle. All of these items are part of the New Mexico Mounted Police Collection. (Fred Lambert.)

JAMES H. McHUGHES. James H. McHughes came to New Mexico to work on the railroad and stayed for the outdoor adventure. Jim worked as a policeman in Santa Fe and Cerrillos. He was an officer in the New Mexico National Guard and was a national champion marksman. Jim joined the mounted police in May 1912 and remained until the force went out of action in late 1913. In later years, Jim operated a small truck farm east of Albuquerque and had amassed a large collection of firearms at the time of his death. (Fred Lambert.)

JOHNSON-FLYNN PRIZEFIGHT TICKET LINE. On Thursday, July 4, 1912, East Las Vegas, New Mexico, was the site of the heavyweight world boxing championship match between "Fireman Jim" Flynn and the champion Jack Johnson. The fight was staged in a specially constructed ring on a vacant lot at what is now the corner of Friedman and Sixth Streets. Flynn had used the Montezuma

Resort as his training facility, and Johnson had a training camp a few blocks north of the Old Town Plaza on Gonzales Street. The governor ordered the mounted police to be at the fight to maintain order to enforce the new state's prizefight law. (Fred Lambert.)

JOHNSON-FLYNN PRIZEFIGHT TICKET. Captain Fornoff was ordered by Governor McDonald to take charge of the law enforcement ringside. The rangers had been ordered to stop the fight at the conclusion of the ninth round if a winner had not already been determined. Disregarding the referee, ring officials, and the crowd of thousands, Fornoff and his men enforced the law. A motion picture company filmed the contest, and even a casual observer can identify Fornoff as he stepped into the ring followed by his men. (Fred Lambert.)

STATE SENATOR HERBERT B. HOLT. Herbert Bartlett Holt, an attorney from Las Cruces, had served as a defense counselor for Wayne Brazel, the confessed killer of Pat Garrett, in 1908. Holt was no friend of the mounted police. He believed that they did little more than hang around saloons picking bar fights. As the Republican floor leader in the 1913 session of the First State Legislature, Holt led the senate fight to abolish the mounted police as a waster of taxpayer money. The governor threatened to veto any legislation to disband the state police. Holt led a new effort to prohibit funding for the rangers. He won the allocation battle. (*New Mexico Blue Book*, 1913.)

TERRITORIAL/STATE AUDITOR WILLIAM
G. SARGENT, 1901–1918. The Mounted
Police Act of 1905 mandated that the
territorial auditor levy a tax to support
the operation of the rangers. William
G. Sargent, the auditor, took a high-
handed approach by authorizing the
territorial treasurer to pay the expenses
of the new police force. The dispute
was finally settled by a ruling issued by
Atty. Gen. George W. Prichard when
he agreed with Captain Fullerton's
broad view on the funding issue. In
1913, Sargent would again tangle with
rangers concerning mounted police
funding. (Cipriana Baca Randolph.)

STATE EX REL V. SARGENT
18 NM 272. Francis
C. Wilson, president of
the New Mexico Bar
Association, represented
the mounted police in their
lawsuit against the state
auditor. The legal action
was designed to force the
auditor to authorize the
mounted police tax levy
to fund the rangers for the
new fiscal year starting
on December 1, 1913.
The Santa Fe District
Court upheld the police's
position, but Sargent
applied the lower court
ruling to the New Mexico
State Supreme Court
who reversed the district
court. The high court
refused Wilson's request
for a rehearing. (New
Mexico State Records
Center and Archives.)

FRED FORNOFF, CAPITALIST. When the mounted police were refused funding in 1913, Fred Fornoff devoted his time to his former sideline business interests. Since 1911, Fornoff and his two partners, Julius Meyer, a former ranger, and Earl Scott, the Estancia Bank's cashier, had been operating a wholesale salt business. The men had leased a salt lake east of Estancia from the New Mexico Fuel and Iron Company and sold the evaporated by-product of the water. Now Fornoff took an active interest in the business. Captain Fornoff also did some work for the state's tax commission, and he still worked as the chief of detectives for the Santa Fe Central Railroad. This picture shows Fornoff's automobile stuck in the mud while he was on an inspection trip for the tax commission in 1914. (Fred Fornoff Jr.)

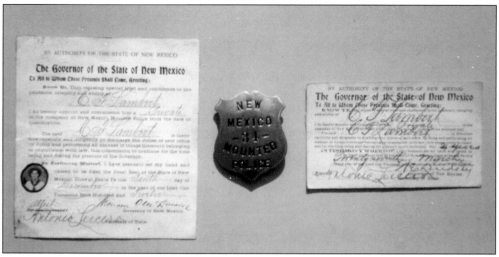

ADDITIONAL AND SPECIAL MOUNTED POLICE. The mounted police reorganization legislation of 1909 reduced the size of the force from 11 men to six and abolished the rank of lieutenant. The new law authorized the governor to appoint additional rangers to serve at his pleasure with or without payment from the territory or state. These additional or special mounted police officers wore a numbered shield identifying them as a ranger. (Fred Lambert.)

SPECIAL MOUNTED POLICE: WILLIAM A. "BILLY" OLD. William A. "Billy" Old was the only man to have served in each of the three southwest ranger forces. He started as a member of the Frontier Battalion in Texas and then served in the Arizona Rangers from 1904 until they were disbanded in 1909; he was the rangers' lieutenant. Old moved to New Mexico to work as a special agent for the Santa Fe Railroad and on July 30, 1910, was appointed a mounted police without pay from the territory.

SPECIAL MOUNTED POLICE: D. R. "DEE" HARKEY. Daniel R. "Dee" Harkey served in numerous peace officer positions. He was a cattle association inspector when, in April 1909, he received the first special mounted police commission issued. In his self-glorifying autobiography, he denigrates two real mounted police tough guys, Fred Higgins and Cicero Stewart, to enhance his own status as the man who "has been shot at more times than any man in the world not engaged in war." (D. R. Harkey.)

SPECIAL MOUNTED POLICE: LORENZO D. WALTERS. Lorenzo D. Walters served in the 6th Cavalry in the early 1890s and was discharged in New Mexico were he went to work for the Bar Cross Cattle Company. He became a special agent for the Santa Fe Railroad in 1908 and was given a special mounted police commission in 1909. Walters moved to Arizona and became a Tucson policeman. He wrote *Tombstone's Yesterday, True Chronicles of Early Arizona. (Tucson Citizen.)*

SPECIAL MOUNTED POLICE: MALAQUIAS BACA. Malaquias Baca was a man of many trades. He was a justice of the peace, a land speculator, postmaster of Roy, a notary public, and a representative from Union County to the 1921 session of the Fifth State Legislature. It is ironic that Baca, who served twice as a ranger, voted to abolish the mounted police. In August 1911, Malaquias Baca was given a 60-day commission as an additional mounted police, with pay, to hunt down a gang of cattle rustlers. The men were captured by mounted policeman Fred Lambert. Baca was given a second mounted police appointment in October 1920. He was named a special mounted police without pay. During this time, Baca won election to the state legislature. (*New Mexico Blue Book,* 1921.)

SPECIAL MOUNTED POLICE: JANDON R. "CHIEF" GALUSHA. Jandon R. Galusha worked for the Santa Fe Railroad as a special agent and was named a special mounted police in November 1910 and served the railroad and the territory until the rangers were disbanded in 1913. Galusha earned his nickname by serving a decade as the chief of police for the city of Albuquerque before becoming the federal adult probation officer for New Mexico. He served until 1956. (Howard Bryan.)

Four

FATHOM FORCE
1913–1918

It would appear at first glance from reading contemporary newspaper stories concerning the funding battle in the state legislature that the New Mexico Mounted Police rode into history on December 1, 1913, but a closer examination of the records tells a different story. Yes the state police lost the appropriation battle, but the legal foundation for the mounted police remained in the law. The Mounted Police Fund also remained intact and contained a sizable amount of money when it was absorbed into the general fund in 1923.

Governor McDonald used the mounted police law to his advantage. It gave him the authority to appoint a ranger to perform a certain task or service for a designated period of time. The appointment could be made with or without salary or per diem from the state.

Fred Lambert moved to Santa Fe in December 1913 and worked as a special officer of the U.S. Indian Service, but Governor McDonald also continued his mounted police commission and used Fred as his man for select special investigations for the state. Captain Fornoff and Jim McHughes also worked as special rangers during 1914. The governor was biding time until the lawmakers returned in session in 1915. He hoped the new legislative session would restore the mounted police appropriation.

The 1915 legislative session continued the status quo and passed the mounted police matter to the next set of legislators in 1917. Fornoff and McHughes took regular jobs and forgot about the mounted police.

Governor McDonald and his two successors continued with Lambert as the lone New Mexico ranger, giving him special assignments and paying him from their contingency fund.

STATE GOVERNOR WILLIAM C. MCDONALD. William Calhoun McDonald was elected the first governor of the state of New Mexico in November 1911 and took office, after statehood was proclaimed on January 6, 1912, at an inauguration ceremony held on January 15. McDonald was a Democrat in a strongly Republican state. Under terms of the new state constitution, McDonald served until January 1, 1917. McDonald was a native of Jordanville, New York. He came to New Mexico as a lawyer but worked as a land surveyor before becoming manager of the Carrizozo Cattle Company in Lincoln County. McDonald later bought the ranch operation. He married a widower with four children, and they had another child together. Governor McDonald was a strong supporter of the mounted police, and he was especially fond of Fred Lambert. The two men were like father and son. McDonald died a few months after leaving office and was buried in White Oaks, now a mining ghost town. (Fred Lambert.)

STATE GOVERNOR E. C. DE BACA. Gov. Ezequiel Cabeza de Baca, a Democrat, was ill when he took office and governed from his sick bed for 49 days in 1917. He never lived in the executive mansion or used the governor's office. De Baca had been the editor of the *La Voz del Pueblo*, the newspaper owned by his family and published in Las Vegas. The newspaper had been anti-mounted police during the funding debate of 1913. (Museum of New Mexico.)

STATE GOVERNOR WASHINGTON E. LINDSEY. Washington Ellsworth Lindsey was a Chicago lawyer for 10 years before he settled in Portales, New Mexico, as a U.S. Commissioner (judge) for New Mexico Territory. He was instrumental in the creation of Roosevelt County and once served as mayor of Portales. His wife was a leader in the temperance movement. Governor Lindsey's Republican administration was honest, effective, patriotic, and worthy of the man. He was a strong voice in support of the need for the wartime mounted police and especially the efforts of Fred Lambert prior to that era. (Museum of New Mexico.)

CAP FORNOFF, TAX COMMISSION AGENT.
Following the conclusion of the 1915 legislative session, Captain Fornoff took a full-time job with the state tax commission. This agency was responsible for an honest assessment of the taxable value of property in the state. Fornoff was able to add thousands of acres to the tax rolls by diligent field work. This newspaper characterization of Fornoff is a good likeness of the man. One might notice that Fornoff is wearing spats over his shoes and developing a paunch. (Fred Fornoff Jr.)

FRED AND KATIE LAMBERT ON MOTORCYCLE PATROL. The photograph shows Fred and Katie Lambert riding on Tesuque Hill north of Santa Fe in 1914. Lambert called his Indian model motorcycle his "motor pony." He was working as a special officer of the U.S. Indian Service, Department of the Interior, for the suppression of liquor sales on Native American lands. He was stationed at Santa Fe and was also a mounted police. (Fred Lambert.)

FRED LAMBERT IN SUIT AND BADGE. This photograph shows Fred Lambert in a ranger uniform and wearing the badge issued to the special mounted police. He is also carrying his Winchester .25-20 carbine. (Fred Lambert.)

MEXICAN RAIDERS IN 1916. The turmoil along the United States-Mexico border reached a fever pitch in 1916, and only a small incident could ignite a ragging inferno. The incident happened in the predawn hours on Thursday, March 9, in the Village of Columbus, New Mexico, and the neighboring U.S. Army camp. The village and the military camp were located in Luna County, a few miles north of the international border. Members of Francisco "Poncho" Villa's ragtag army of Mexican revolutionaries seeking weapons and supplies raided the area. (Fred Lambert.)

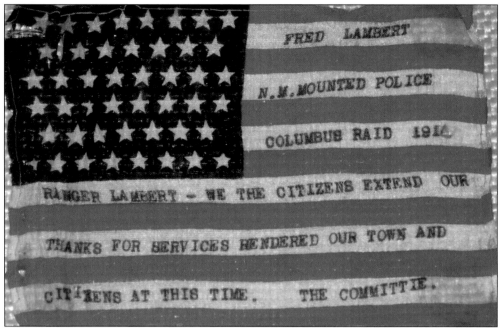

Columbus Raid Flag of Thanks, 1916. Governor McDonald sent Fred Lambert to Columbus to help Luna County officers restore civil order and to act as an information source for the governor. A week later, Gen. John J. "Black Jack" Pershing had assembled 5,000 men of the regular army at Columbus to begin a primitive expedition into Mexico in pursuit of Villa. The entire New Mexico National Guard replaced Pershing's command on May 12, 1916. This small 46-star U.S. flag was a thank you from the citizens of Columbus for Lambert's help in restoring law and order in the community. (Fred Lambert.)

Special New Mexico Mounted Police, 1916–1918. The constant public skirmishes between the different Mexican revolutionary forces along the wide-open range country bordering Northern Mexico, and mounted policeman Lambert's reports concerning the border unrest, caused Governor McDonald to authorize the three border county sheriffs to organize volunteer corps of outstanding citizens to serve as minutemen posses with state police powers. (NMMP.)

U.S. Sen. Thomas Benton Catron. Thomas Benton Catron came to New Mexico following the Civil War and became a skillful leader in Republican party politics. He was the driving force behind the infamous Santa Fe Ring of opportunistic business friends. He used his influence to build his personal wealth by acquiring interest in or clear title to 34 Mexican land grants totalling nearly 3 million acres. Catron's son, Charles Christopher, managed much of his father's land grant operations. Fred Lambert became manager of the Ojo Del Espiritu Santo Grant in July 1915 and operated the 113,000 acres until early 1917. This was his "day job" as Governor McDonald continued to request his investigative skills for the state rangers. (Fred Lambert.)

STATE SENATOR RAMON SANCHEZ. Ramon Sanchez owned a mercantile store at Penasco in Taos County. Five days before Christmas 1916, the newly elected state senator received a demand for $1,000 payable by January 1 upon the pain of death. The blackmail note was accompanied by rifle shots through the front door of Sanchez's home. Governor McDonald ordered Fred Lambert to handle the case. Two days later, during a blinding snowstorm, Lambert rode into Penasco. (*New Mexico Blue Book,* 1919.)

BLACKMAIL CASE, 1917. Mounted policeman Fred Lambert discovered that the death threats against state senator Ramon Sanchez had been written in green ink on line paper from a school tablet. On his second day impersonating a school census taker, Lambert discovered the source of both the ink and the paper. A few days later, Lambert arrested Felix Sanchez, a second cousin to the senator, as the blackmailer. This blackmail incident proved to be Fred Lambert's last case as a New Mexico Mounted Police. (Fred Lambert.)

Five

WARTIME RANGERS
1918

On Saturday, April 1, 1916, Governor McDonald used the authority vested in him under Section 5412 of the New Mexico Statutes Annotated 1915 to appoint special members of the New Mexico Mounted Police to service without remuneration from the state by assisting the three border sheriffs maintain security. This first group of 274 men was given 60-day ranger commissions. Governor McDonald added 39 more men to his special state police on May 29 with an additional 70 men added on June 1 and a final 25 men a week later. These last three groups received six-month appointments. The process continued during 1917, and by 1918, over a thousand special mounted police commissions had been issued.

The State Council of Defense for New Mexico found it necessary to re-establish the New Mexico Mounted Police as a fully funded state agency on account of the continuing troubled conditions along the United States-Mexico border during the spring of 1918. A three-member state police committee developed a set of rules and regulations to govern the new nonpartisan ranger company. The governor appointed Herb McGrath as the captain of the 17-man force with their headquarters in Silver City.

The State Council of Defense and the Cattle Sanitary Board jointly provided the operational funding for a captain, two sergeants, and 14 privates. The wartime rangers were authorized to operate from May 1 to December 31, 1918. There was a provision that the governor could extend the length of the operation if the need for the force was exceeded.

During the eight months that Captain McGrath's wartime rangers operated, they made 452 arrests for crimes ranging from murder to bootlegging, from prostitution to burglary, wartime crimes, and violation of the state's motor vehicle laws.

B. C. HERNANDEZ. Benigno C. Hernandez of Tierra Amarilla was one of the key leaders of the State Council of Defense that had been established by the special session of the Third State Legislature in April 1917. Hernandez was a supporter of the mounted police concept. He had asked for and received assistance from Fullerton's Rangers during a difficult murder investigation when he was the Rio Arriba County sheriff in 1905. (*History of New Mexico*, 1907.)

WALTER M. DANBURG, GENERAL SECRETARY. The New Mexico State Council of Defense was established in May 1917 and functioned until May 1920. Walter M. Danburg was named the general secretary for the council in October 1917 and conducted the day-to-day operation until the disbandment of the council. Danburg was a strong administrator and fiscal manager. He supported the mission of the mounted police during and after the wartime service. (*New Mexico Blue Book*, 1919.)

SPANISH FLU PANDEMIC OF 1918. Capt. Herb McGrath's newly reorganized New Mexico Mounted Police hunted livestock thieves, draft dodgers, price-gouging merchants, border "alien terrorist" and saboteurs, prohibition offenders, and automobile law violators. These wartime rangers also fought an unseen menses—the Spanish flu. The worldwide pandemic dominated newspaper headlines and editorial cartoons, like this one from the *Dallas Morning News* cartoonist John Knott. (*Dallas Morning News* Archives.)

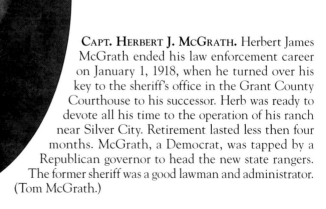

CAPT. HERBERT J. MCGRATH. Herbert James McGrath ended his law enforcement career on January 1, 1918, when he turned over his key to the sheriff's office in the Grant County Courthouse to his successor. Herb was ready to devote all his time to the operation of his ranch near Silver City. Retirement lasted less then four months. McGrath, a Democrat, was tapped by a Republican governor to head the new state rangers. The former sheriff was a good lawman and administrator. (Tom McGrath.)

OLDER FRED FORNOFF. Capt. Herb McGrath asked former mounted police leader Fred Fornoff to recommend and help recruit the right men to compose the new corps of rangers. Fornoff selected a few of his former rangers and a group of younger veterans. One man that Governor Lindsey, Captain McGrath, and Fornoff wanted to be part of the reorganized mounted police was Fred Lambert. (Fred Fornoff Jr.)

CIPRIANO BACA. Cipriano Baca was another former ranger that was actively recruited to return to the rangers. Baca was working as a deputy sheriff and mine guard in Madrid. He accepted the offer to ride again with the mounted police. The photograph of Cipriano Baca on horseback was taken in front of the Grant County Courthouse. Baca was always ready for action. (Cipriana Baca Randolph.)

FRED AND KATIE LAMBERT IN MISSOURI. Fred Lambert was unable to accept the invitation to ride with the wartime rangers. He and Katie were living in the Kansas City area. He was helping Katie's ailing brother operate his livestock commission sales business. The Lamberts returned to New Mexico in the 1920s. One might note that Lambert is wearing his mounted police star in this picture. (Fred Lambert.)

FRED LAMBERT AND THE AUTHOR, 1970. The author first met Fred Lambert in the summer of 1967, and the relationship grew over the years. The author was the grandson that Lambert never had, and Lambert was the mentor that a young man needed. Lambert set the author on a 40-year quest to discover the true tale of the New Mexico Mounted Police and to write about their colorful history.

FRED LAMBERT WITH NAMESAKE AND AUTHOR'S WIFE. This picture was taken at the author's birthday celebration in June 1969. The party was held at Lambert's home in Cimarron, New Mexico. The old lawman is holding the author's eldest son, Scott Lambert Hornung, named in his honor. Lambert acted as Scott's godfather. They are accompanied by V. J., the author's wife. Fred was always glad to see both of them. Lambert did the pen-and-ink drawings and the many oil paintings hanging on the wall in the background.

FRED LAMBERT IN OLD AGE. Fred Lambert spent his last years living in a small cottage near the Old Mill Museum in Cimarron, New Mexico. The dwelling is owned by the CS Cattle Company. It was provided by the owner, Les Davis, as a place for Lambert to live while he operated the museum as curator and tour host. In this picture, Fred is looking at his favorite picture of his beloved wife, Katie, who died in 1964. He missed her everyday for the rest of his life.

Six

THE REORGANIZED STATE MOUNTED POLICE
1919–1921

The New Mexico Mounted Police was raised from the grave and reorganized for a third time on January 3, 1919. The newly inaugurated governor, O. A. Larrazolo, understood the need for the mounted police and ordered the New Mexico State Council of Defense to continue to fund the rangers.

A. A. Sena, one of Fornoff's former rangers, was selected to head the new company. Las Vegas was selected as the new mounted police headquarters city, and an office was acquired on Bridge Street between the Old Town Plaza and the newer East Las Vegas. The new headquarters even had a telephone number connected to the long distance line.

During 1919 and 1920, the 20-man ranger force arrested 716 offenders. There is no record that the rangers made any arrest during their one-month operation during 1921. The force, operated by Captain Sena, had a $50,000 annual budget.

STATE GOVERNOR OCTAVIANO A. LARRAZOLO. Octaviano Ambrosio Larrazolo was born in the State of Chihuahua, Mexico, in 1860, and he died in New Mexico in April 1930. He practiced law in El Paso and Las Vegas, New Mexico, and became a public servant in both communities. Following his term as governor, Larrazolo finally won a seat in the U.S. House of Representatives in 1926. He won a U.S. Senate seat in 1928, but due to ill health, he served only a few months and returned to Albuquerque. Larrazolo supported the need for the mounted police and used his power as the commander in chief to order the rangers to coal country to break up the miner's strike at Gallup in 1919. This action cost the rangers their hard-earned goodwill among the working class people of the state. (Museum of New Mexico.)

STATE GOVERNOR MERRITT C. MECHEM. Merritt Cramer Mechem was born in Ottawa, Kansas, in October 1870 and grew up and was educated as a cornhusker. Mechem settled in Tucumcari in 1903 and opened a law office. He served as a territorial judge and became a district court judge after statehood. He was elected governor on the Republican's 1920 fiscal reform platform. Mechem was friends with a few of the men who had served in the mounted police under captains Fullerton and Fornoff, but was not a strong supporter of the new organization as operated by Captain Sena. (Museum of New Mexico.)

CAPT. APOLONIO A. SENA.
Apolonio A. Sena was a man of opportunity. He worked as a teacher, rancher, probate clerk, city alderman, mail contractor, county tax assessor, hotel manager, newspaper editor, bill collector, and justice of the peace. He also served as a ranger under Fred Fornoff. Sena served as a county sheriff and a deputy U.S. marshal. In late 1920, Sena resigned his mounted police commission and started his campaign for the U.S. Senate. He lost. (*History of New Mexico*, 1907.)

SANTA ROSA RICO, NMMP.
Santa Rosa Rico was a native New Mexican. In the early 1880s, he served as a wagon train scout and was the only survivor of an Apache attack near Lordsburg. For nearly four decades, his cousins Jose and Felipe Lucero served as the chief lawmen in Dona Ana County. Rico served as a constable or deputy sheriff before becoming a railroad policeman and a special mounted police in the summer of 1913. On July 3, 1919, Rico took his oath as a full-time mounted police, serving at Las Cruces. He was reappointed in 1920 and served under captains Sena and Delgado until the force was disbanded in February 1921. The Mounted Police Department arrest records bear witness that mounted policeman Rico was an effective officer. (NMMP.)

THE LAST COMPANY, 1921. The few remaining pieces of official records of the New Mexico Mounted Police from 1921 are written upon Sena's stationary. The former captain's name is crossed out and "L. Delgado" is inked in that place. Governor Mechem named Lorenzo Delgado as captain of the mounted police on January 7, 1921, to "serve at the pleasure of the governor." The commission would have been more accurate had it said at the "pleasure of the legislature," because the office, in fact the whole force, was abolished on February 15, 1921. Delgado was the mounted police captain for 36 days. In 1920, the legislature's ad hoc revenue commission, chaired by former governor Herbert J. Hagerman, made nine recommendations on how to strengthen the state's budget-to-revenue ratio. One of these recommendations was to "abolish superfluous offices," and one of the departments on the list was the mounted police. The plan replaced the 20-man ranger force with a four-man state marshal's agency to save money. Governor Mechem ran for governor on the Republican party platform that embraced the revenue commission's report. He was bound to sign any bill that was passed to enact the features of the tax reduction-spending plan. Lorenzo Delgado had been promised that he would be appointed as the chief state marshal if the mounted police were abolished. The police were killed as expected, but the plan to give life to the state marshals never happened. In a twisted irony of fate, Delgado served as the chief clerk of the House of Representatives in 1921 when they abolished the mounted police and neglected to enact the state marshal proposal.

Capt. Lorenzo Delgado. Lorenzo Delgado was a born politician and had a reputation as a Don Juan, which he used to mask his sooth political manner. He was lifelong bachelor. Delgado had once been a business partner with A. A. Sena in a coal, wool, and grain wholesale company. He was also a horse and cattle rancher. Delgado was a highly successful mayor of Las Vegas, and as sheriff of San Miguel County he ran the Ku Klux Klan out of his jurisdiction. He even cultivated the political support of the ultra-religious Penitente movement. (*History of New Mexico*, 1907.)

State Peace Officer Identification Card, 1921. When the New Mexico Mounted Police was abolished, it was realized that railroad companies no longer had a way for their special agents or detectives to exercise police power across county jurisdictions. In the closing days of the 1921 legislative session, Council Bill 193 was introduced and given a quick rush through the lawmaking process. Governor Mechem signed the bill into law on March 12, 1921. (Gov. M. C. Mechem Papers.)

CHAPTER 141.

An Act to Provide for the Appointment of Peace Officers

to Serve Upon the Premises or Property of Railroad Companies.

S. B. No. 193; Approved March 12, 1921.

Be It Enacted by the Legislature of the State of New Mexico:

Section 1. The Governor of this State is hereby auth̲o̲r̲i̲z̲e̲d̲ and empowered, upon the applicati̲o̲n̲ ̲o̲f̲ to appoint, and to commis̲s̲ one or more persons design̲a̲ sole expense of such comp̲ powers of regular peace of̲ ficient bond to the State o̲ Five Thousand Dollars ($5̲ ance of their duties. The or persons shall be responsi̲ their authority; Provided, tha̲ shall not have authority as s̲ or to be used as peace officers̲ troubles.

Sec. 2. That it is necess̲ public peace and safety of the̲ Mexico that the provisions of th̲ the earliest possible time, and, th̲.̲.̲.̲.̲.̲,̲ all emergency is here-by declared to exist, and this act shall take effect and be in full force and effect from and after its passage and approval.

BY AUTHORITY OF THE STATE OF NEW MEXICO

The Governor of the State of New Mexico

To All to Whom These Presents Shall Come, meeting:

KNOW YE that, reposing special trust and confidence in the integrity, ability and discretion of *J. B. Kelly*

I do hereby commission him as PEACE OFFICER in the State of New Mexico, with all the powers of regular peace officers, to serve upon the property of Railroad Companies, without pay from the State of New Mexico, and during the pleasure of the Governor.

Done at Santa Fe, N. M., this 4th day of April 1922

M. C. Mechem
GOVERNOR

Attest:
SECRETARY OF STATE

Seven

THE NEW MEXICO MOUNTED POLICE

RECORDS AND EQUIPMENT

The New Mexico State Records Center and Archives in Santa Fe is the custodian of the official records of the New Mexico Mounted Police. They are not contained in one single collection but are filed among the records of many agencies. Most of the territorial police records are stored in a few boxes composed of correspondence and weekly reports, a few case files, a carton of prisoner arrest cards, and a couple of scrapbooks that contained wanted notices. The state ranger documents are stored with the records of the State Council of Defense and in the papers of the governor who commissioned the men who served his administration. Small files of mounted police–related documents are also located in the records of other government agencies.

The author has discovered, over 40 years of research, that some of the rangers' descendents have records and equipment that their ancestor had retained when he left the rangers. The largest private collection of mounted police memorabilia was collected by Fred Lambert and today is the cornerstone of the author's New Mexico Mounted Police Collection.

NEW MEXICO MOUNTED POLICE COMMISSION, 1905. This is the large wall-size commission given to John F. Fullerton on March 18, 1905, when he was appointed by Gov. Miguel A. Otero as the first captain of the mounted police. The official seal and the ribbon are intact after more than a century. (Susan Leverett.)

TERRITORY OF NEW MEXICO,
County of _Santa Fe_ } ss.

I, _Rafael Gomez_, born in _the County of Socorro, N. Mex_ in the _year 1866_, aged _39_ years, and _11 months_, and by occupation a _laborer_, do hereby acknowledge to have voluntarily enlisted (or re-enlisted), on this _14th_ day of _December_, A. D. 190_5_, in the National Guard of New Mexico, for the period _ending March 31/06_, unless sooner discharged by proper authority, and I do also agree to accept from the Territory of New Mexico such bounty, pay, rations and clothing as are or may be established by law. And I do solemnly swear (or affirm) that I will bear true faith and allegiance to the United States of America and Territory of New Mexico; that I will serve them honestly and faithfully against all their enemies whomsoever; that I will support the Constitution of the United States and the Laws of the Territory of New Mexico, and that I will obey the orders of the Governor of New Mexico and the Commander-in-Chief of the Military forces thereof, and the orders of the officers appointed over me, according to the rules rmy regulations and articles of war of the United States, so far as they may be applicable under the laws of the Territory of New Mexico, and the laws of said Territory of New Mexico. So help me God.

Rafael Gomez . (SEAL)

Subscribed and sworn to before me this _14th_ day of _December_, A. D. 190_5_.

John T. Fullerton
Recruiting Officer.

NEW MEXICO MOUNTED POLICE OATH OF OFFICE, 1905. The mounted police concept was so new when Capt. John Fullerton enrolled his men on April 1, 1905, that he was forced to use crossed over National Guard muster and oath of office forms. Starting in 1906, and for the rest of their history, the mounted police used the standard territory and state oath of office form for all government employees. These forms are part of the secretary of the territory/state's records. (New Mexico State Records Center and Archives.)

NEW MEXICO MOUNTED POLICE BADGE DESIGN, 1905. Section 14 of the New Mexico Mounted Police Act of 1905 stipulated the captain would provide each ranger with a badge "uniform in size and shape with the words, 'New Mexico Mounted Police' inscribed thereon in plain, legible letters." The officers' shield contained their rank at the top, while the privates' had a number. Records indicate that the badges cost $2 apiece. None of these badges are known to have survived.

NEW MEXICO MOUNTED POLICE STAR. Capt. Fred Fornoff commissioned a Santa Fe silversmith to make a dozen silver-star-shaped badges. Fornoff kept one badge in reserve in case a ranger lost his and needed a replacement. All of the mounted police badges, except one, were recalled in November 1913 in exchange for the ranger's final paycheck. Fred Lambert retained his star since he would continue to function as a ranger working under the direction of the governor. The remaining star badges were destroyed. (NMMP.)

NEW MEXICO MOUNTED POLICE BADGE, 1919–1921. This mounted police badge was identified by Fred Lambert as the style worn by the men who served as rangers under captains A. A. Sena and Lorenzo Delgado between January 1919 and January 1921. This badge is in a private collection. (Ron Donaho.)

WINCHESTER .30-40 M1895. Captain Fullerton was a sportsman and championed the Winchester 95, the brainchild of gun designer John M. Browning, as the standard long gun of his rangers. The rifle was liver action with a five-round box magazine for the new steel jacketed or soft nosed lead .30-40-caliber smokeless power cartridges. Some of these rifles were still in use by the state police in 1930s. (Sears Roebuck and Company Catalogue, 1902.)

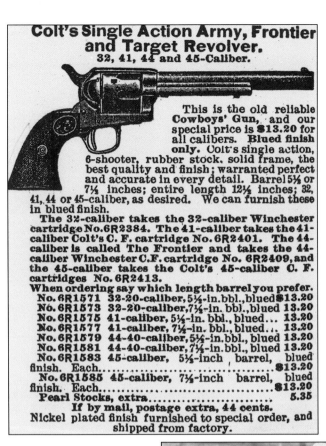

Colt's Single Action Army, Frontier and Target Revolver.
32, 41, 44 and 45-Caliber.

This is the old reliable Cowboys' Gun, and our special price is $13.20 for all calibers. Blued finish only. Colt's single action, 6-shooter, rubber stock, solid frame, the best quality and finish; warranted perfect and accurate in every detail. Barrel 5½ or 7½ inches; entire length 12½ inches; 32, 41, 44 or 45-caliber, as desired. We can furnish these in blued finish.

The 32-caliber takes the 32-caliber Winchester cartridge No. 6R2384. The 41-caliber takes the 41-caliber Colt's C. F. cartridge No. 6R2401. The 44-caliber is called The Frontier and takes the 44-caliber Winchester C.F. cartridge No. 6R2409, and the 45-caliber takes the Colt's 45-caliber C. F. cartridges No. 6R2413.

When ordering say which length barrel you prefer.

No. 6R1571 32-20-caliber, 5½-in. bbl., blued $13.20
No. 6R1573 32-20-caliber, 7½-in. bbl., blued 13.20
No. 6R1575 41-caliber, 5½-in. bbl., blued... 13.20
No. 6R1577 41-caliber, 7½-in. bbl., blued... 13.20
No. 6R1579 44-40-caliber, 5½-in. bbl., blued 13.20
No. 6R1581 44-40-caliber, 7½-in. bbl., blued 13.20
No. 6R1583 45-caliber, 5½-inch barrel, blued finish. Each................................$13.20
No. 6R1585 45-caliber, 7½-inch barrel, blued finish. Each................................$13.20
Pearl Stocks, extra..........................5.35
If by mail, postage extra, 44 cents.
Nickel plated finish furnished to special order, and shipped from factory.

COLT .45 FRONTIER MODEL. Section 4 of the Mounted Police Act of 1905 said that each ranger was to be equipped with a "six-shooting pistol [Army size] and all necessary accoutrements." There was no specification as to make or model of the weapon, but the rangers were only supplied .45-caliber ammunition at taxpayers' expense. The most popular handgun on the frontier was the Colt revolver chambered for the .45 or the .44-40. (Sears Roebuck and Company Catalogue, 1902.)

MOUNTED POLICE RAILROAD PASSES. Many of the railroads that operated in New Mexico Territory supported the establishment of the mounted police and provided free transportation for them and their equipment. The presence of the rangers on a train had a calming effect on the rougher class of travelers and provided a feeling of security for the passengers. The federal government prohibited rail passes in 1907, and this unbudgeted transportation cost crippled the mobility of the rangers to the speed of a horse. (Steve Meyer.)

Posted Aug 26 1907

STOLEN:

Two black horses, 10 years old, star in forehead of each; both wire-scarred on feet, 15 hands high, branded combination ⊄F on left hip. Were hired from J. N. McFate's Livery Barn August 7th, working in light spring-wagon harness with round-top hames and to two horse buggy with leather top, extra wide seat and high bed.

Any information leading to recovery of property and apprehension of the thief will be liberally rewarded.

WM. E. DUDLEY, M. Police.

Alamogordo, N. M., Aug. 19, 1907.

NEW MEXICO MOUNTED POLICE PENNY POSTCARD REWARD NOTICES. Each of the mounted police was authorized to post reward notices for wanted men or stolen livestock. The reward money was provided by the owner of the stolen property or the organization seeking the arrest of an individual criminal. The most economical and useful reward notice was printed on a penny postcard and mailed to law enforcement agencies. (Fred Lambert.)

$200.00 REWARD $200.00

I will pay the above reward for the arrest and conviction of the person who stole a blue horse from my corral in Socorro Saturday night, April 11, sometime after midnight. The horse is branded ⊓ on the right thigh.

R. W. LEWIS.

Socorro, N. M., April 13, 1908.

A PERSONAL REWARD NOTICE. Bob Lewis had one of his own horses stolen in April 1908. He offered a reward for the arrest of the rustler and hopefully the return of the missing horse. Lewis recovered the horse, but the thief was never identified. (Fred Lambert.)

LOSt on night of July 17, 1911 from Rincon, N.M.---- One mare mule 16 hands high, 1200#, 9 yrs/ old new scar on nose, cut on front off fetlock; black mealy nose; no brand.

One mare mule; 16 hands high; 8 yrs. old; 1200#; dark brown; light belly; horse shoe brand left jaw. 15 dollars will be paid for information leading to recovery or $ 25.00 for return to Frank Jennings, Rincon, N.M.

* * * * * * * * * * *

Stolen from Clayton, N.M. about July 15, 1911--- one bay horse; 6 yrs. old; 1050#; long scar on inside of each hind leg; scar on right front leg; had on halter; $ 15.00 reward will be paid for information leading to recovery of horse. D. W. Snyder, Sheriff.

* * * * * * * * * *

Stolen from Silver City, N.M. about July 1, 1911--- one black horse with part of tongue cut away. Some people called it a brown horse, but is never a black. Is branded □ on left shoulder and Ⓖ on right shoulder. Is a good saddler. Send any information to Mr. Geo. H. Bisby, Silver City, N.M. or Fred Fornoff, Santa Fe, N.M.

* * * * * * * * * *

Stolen from Henry Wortman, Peralta, N.M. about July 15, 1911-- one dark brown mare about 5 yrs. old branded as follows: Y on left jaw; PE on left hind leg; SC on right hind leg. Supposed to be taken to the vicinity of Chililli, N.M.

* * * * * * * * * *

Stolen from the ranch of Juan A. Bernal near Arroyo Seco, Taos Co., on the night of July 23, 1911--- one bay horse about 14 hands high; scar on left shoulder. Branded T on left hip.

One blue mare about the same height and braded LA on left shoulder. Has an old wire scar near hoof of right fore foot. One tall dark complected mexican and a smaller light complected man (also mexican-) , the latter wearing a mustache are supposed to be the thieves and are headed for Albuquerque. A reward of $ 50.00 will be paid for the return of the horses.

* * * * * * * * * *

Any information in regard to the above should be addressed to FRED FORNOFF, Captain New Mexico Mounted Police, Santa Fe, N.M.

NEW MEXICO MOUNTED POLICE REWARD NOTICE BULLETIN. As the mounted police became more experienced in search methods, the more effective the organization became in recovering lost property. The mounted police office was soon flooded with reward notices for lost or stolen property. Captain Fornoff devised the weekly "wanted bulletin," which combined all the new notices received at the headquarters and sent this single information sheet to his rangers. (Fred Lambert.)

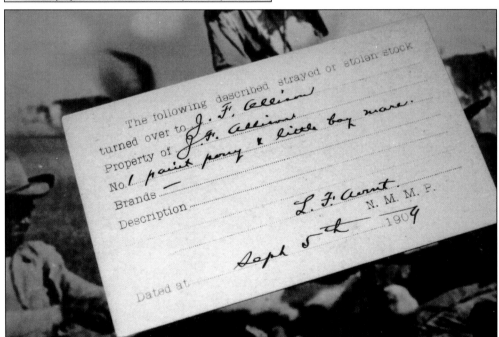

NEW MEXICO MOUNTED POLICE PROPERTY RECOVERY CARD. When the mounted police located stolen property, the ranger was required to fill out a recovery card noting the details of the find and send this information to headquarters. The disposition card was filed to keep a record of the effectiveness of the rangers during that fiscal year. The data was used by Captain Fornoff in his annual report to the governor. (New Mexico State Records Center and Archives.)

CRIMINAL REWARD NOTICES. The mounted police records in the New Mexico State Records Center and Archives contains two large scrapbooks of wanted notices. Most are simple fact sheets containing the information of the crime and the person wanted in connection with the act. A few notices contain a photograph of the wanted individual. Photo reproduction was more expensive in the early 1900s. (New Mexico State Records Center and Archives.)

MOUNTED POLICE CRIMINAL ARREST CARD. Captain Fornoff designed a standard mounted police information card to be used by his rangers for recording the data concerning any individual they arrested. Some of the rangers had this arrest card personalized for their use. (Fred Lambert.)

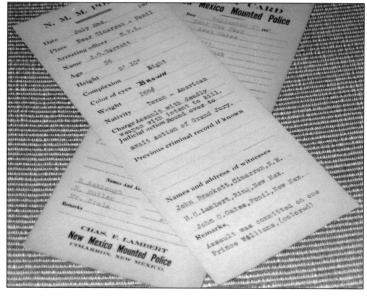

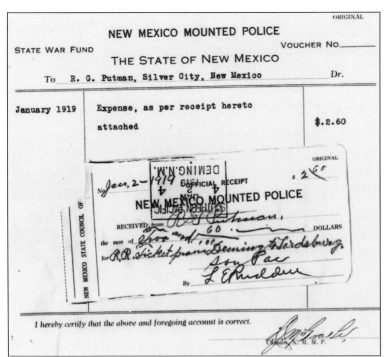

EXPENSE REPORT
AND VOUCHER.
This is an example
of the expense
report and voucher
used by the men
serving under Capt.
Herb McGrath
when the rangers
were paid from the
budget of the State
Council of Defense.
The mounted police
financial records for
these few months
are the most
meticulous spending
documents in
the department
files. (Gov. O. A.
Larrazolo Papers.)

EXAMPLE OF SOME EQUIPMENT USED BY THE MOUNTED POLICE. This photograph contains some of the equipment used by the territorial rangers. The Winchester M1873 was used by Captain Fornoff, the shotgun belonged to Lt. John Collier, and the Colt pistol and homemade holster were part of the arsenal owned by mounted policeman J. B. Rusk. (NMMP.)

CAPTAIN FORNOFF'S PISTOL. This is a picture of a custom engraved Colt .44-40 Model 1878 manufactured in 1894. The handgun was used by Fornoff while he was marshal of Albuquerque. The pistol belongs to a private gun collector.

CAPTAIN FORNOFF'S RIFLE. Captain Fornoff was a man of large stature and liked a heavy rifle. He owned this Winchester .44-40, Model 1873, serial number 473227B. He gave the weapon to Fred Lambert sometime after the mounted police disbanded in December 1913. The two men had a grandfather-grandson relationship. (NMMP.)

CAPTAIN SENA'S PISTOL. This nickel-plated presentation Colt .45, serial number 317839, was given to Apolonio A. Sena when he was a ranger and helped Captain Fornoff and a railroad special agent solve the kidnapping of the grandson of a judge in the spring of 1911. The engraving on the barrel says, "Presented to A. A. Sena by the citizens of Las Vegas New Mexico—April 1911." Captain Fornoff and the detective also received pistols. (Ed Robison.)

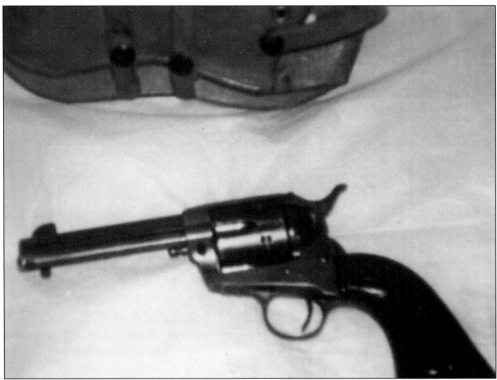

LT. CIPRIANO BACA'S COLT .45 AND PISTOL SCABBARD. Cipriano Baca owned and used many handguns, rifles, and other weapons during his long and distinguished law enforcement career. Two of his weapons are known to still exist. One is this Frontier Model Colt .45 with a 5.5-inch barrel. Baca gave this pistol and holster to his daughter, Cipriana, during their last visit in 1935. The weapon is still owned by members of the Baca family. (Cipriana Baca Randolph.)

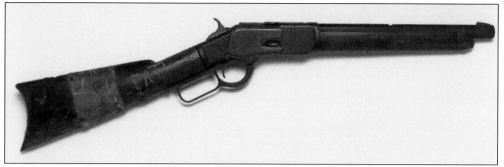

CIPRIANO BACA'S WINCHESTER. Cipriano Baca acquired Winchester .44-40 M1873, serial number 31829, manufactured in 1879, in a poker game with Pat F. Garrett in Deming, New Mexico. Garrett was the regional government custom's agent, and Baca was the county sheriff. Baca gave the rifle to his son, Florentino, when the youth went to live with his uncle in Old Mexico. A few years later, Florentino attended the New Mexico School of Mines at Socorro. He hocked the rifle to a classmate but never retrieved the weapon. (Ruidoso River Museum.)

LT. JOHN COLLIER'S SHOTGUN. This picture shows an Occidental 12-gauge, double-barrel breakdown shotgun, serial number 18493, with a canvas carrying case. Jim McHughes traded Collier for this shotgun to add to his weapons collections. In the spring of 1933, McHughes gave the shotgun once owned by "Ole Windjammer John" Collier to Fred Lambert as a thank you for a copy of Fred's book of poetry and pen-and-ink drawings called *Bunkhouse Tales of Wild Horse Charley.* (NMMP.)

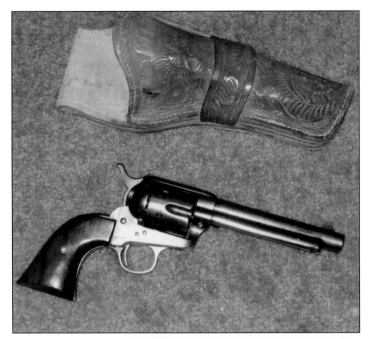

J. B. "Slim" Rusk's Colt .38-40. Pictured is one of J. B. "Slim" Rusk's pistols. Rusk had a collection of different-style weapons that he used during his career as a peace officer. This is a Colt .38-40 Peacemaker Model, serial number 228926, manufactured in 1902. Rusk gave the weapon to Fred Lambert while the two men were working a case together in October 1911. Lambert had lost his pistol while chasing a suspected rustler, so Rusk let Lambert have his backup weapon. (NMMP.)

Fred Lambert's Pistol and Badge. This Colt .32-20 is a custom factory-engraved Frontier model with pearl-handled ox head grips. The weapon has a 5.5-inch barrel and the serial number 305332. The badges in the case represent the law enforcement positions Lambert held during his 50-year career. Lambert's relatives sold individual badges to collectors following Fred's death.

104

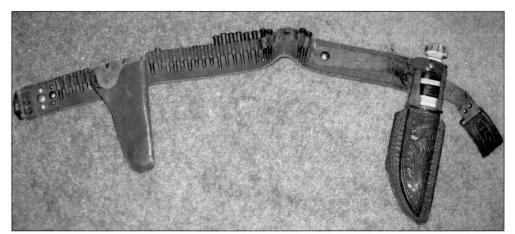

FRED LAMBERT'S GUN BELT. This a picture of the cartridge belt and pistol scabbard worn by Fred Lambert. The hunting knife with the bone handle was given to Lambert by one of his Native American deputies. The belt contains loops for ten .25-35 rifle cartridges and fourteen .32-20 pistol cartridges. (NMMP.)

FRED LAMBERT'S WINCHESTER. This Winchester .25-35, Model 1894, smokeless power cartridge saddle carbine was owned and used by Fred Lambert. It was manufactured in 1909 and is stamped with serial number 429934. The Sheldon-Payne Arms Company in El Paso made the saddle rifle scabbard. (NMMP.)

MOUNTED POLICE WEAPONS. The current version of the New Mexico state flag serves as the backdrop for Captain Fornoff's Winchester rifle, Lt. John Collier's shotgun, J. B. Rusk's Colt pistol, and Fred Lambert's Winchester saddle carbine. This New Mexico state flag covered the coffin of Fred Lambert as his body lay in state and at the graveside service in February 1971. (NMMP.)

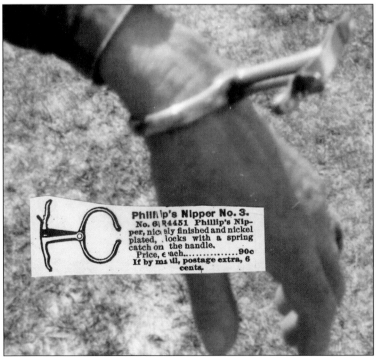

"COME ALONG, OR TWISTER-NIPPER. The mounted police used the Nipper, sometimes called a "Come Along" or Twister, to assist in transporting a handcuffed prisoner. This issue was patent in 1892. (NMMP.)

MOUNTED POLICE HANDCUFFS. The model of handcuff was patent in 1890 and was popular with the mounted police because of its strength and dependability. (NMMP.)

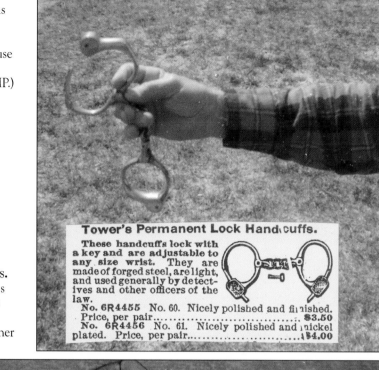

MOUNTED POLICE PRISONER RESTRAINTS. This picture illustrates the array of restraints used by the mounted police to keep a prisoner in custody. (NMMP.)

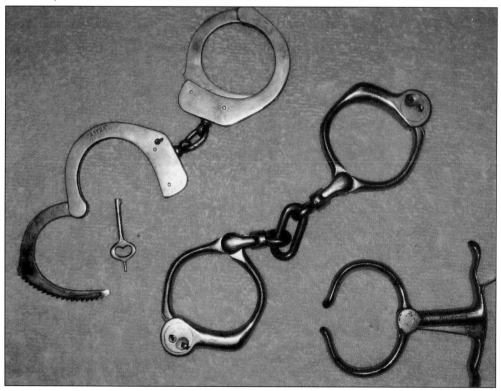

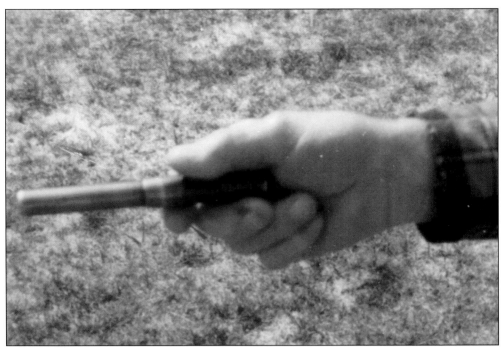

THE GAS PISTOL. In this picture, Fred Lambert is demonstrating the proper use of a "gas pistol" he employed to clear a saloon of unruly customers. The weapon was the forerunner the present-day tear gas canister. (NMMP.)

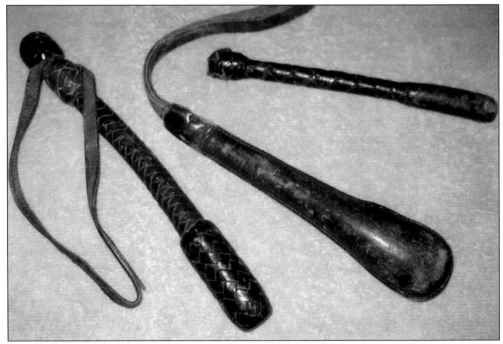

BLACKJACKS OR "TAPERS." The blackjack or "taper" was a common weapon used by frontier lawmen to subdue a prisoner. The middle blackjack in this picture was used by Fred Lambert during his arrest of the "badman," Profecto Cordova, in 1912. (NMMP.)

FRED LAMBERT'S FIELD GLASSES. These are the French made field glasses used by Fred Lambert while he served as a member of the mounted police. Both the glasses and the case show signs of hard usage. (NMMP.)

CAMP GEAR. This picture shows a Spanish-American War–era mess kit used by the mounted police while on scout duty. Also shown is a silver folding drinking cup and a knife and fork set. The food was typical of that eaten by the rangers—a baked potato, slice of beef, and a flour tortilla. (NMMP.)

DRINKING CUP AND WHISTLE. The collapsible drinking cup became very popular in the 1890s and was used by campers and people involved in a new sport craze—bicycling. The standard police whistle was used for signaling to fellow officers. (NMMP.)

SAVING SOAP AND RAZOR. These were Fred Lambert's straight razor and shaving mug that he used at home or in the field on scout duty. (NMMP.)

CANTEEN. The canteen was very important to a mounted police while working on scout duty. The surplus military canteens from the Spanish-American War of 1898 were popular in frontier New Mexico. They were cheap, and a pack animal could carry a few of these in a field pack. (NMMP.)

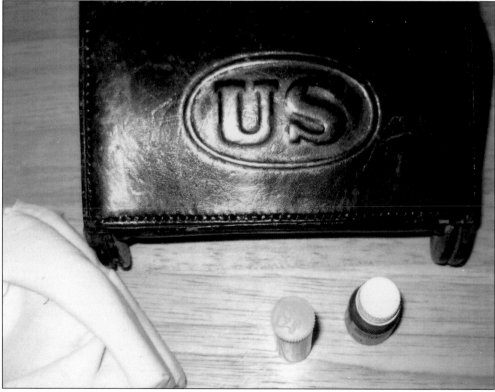

FIRST AID KIT. The military ammunition belt pack was often converted into a first aid kit that could be easily carried on the saddle. Note that Fred Lambert's self-portrait pen-and-ink drawing shows this pack on his saddle horn (see page 60). (NMMP.)

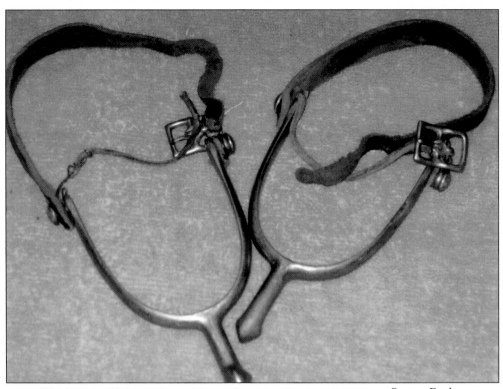

SPURS. Fred Lambert wore simple spurs while on scout duty so that he made no unnecessary noise while trailing a fugitive. (NMMP.)

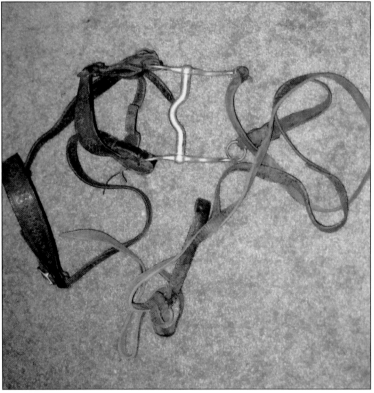

HORSE BRIDLE. This is the bridle that Fred Lambert used with his favorite mount, a pinto pony he called Wallo-K-Whoop. The two traveled many trails together. (NMMP.)

MOUNTED POLICE FORD FLIVVER, 1918. The executive committee of New Mexico's State Council of Defense authorized Captain McGrath to buy a Ford Model T Flivver for the use of his headquarters' staff stationed at Silver City. The council paid $521.05 for the automobile. About a year after its original purchase, the Ford Flivver was sold for $200, less storage fees and repair bills. The Council of Defense received a check for $150 from the Ford dealership in Silver City for the very well used vehicle.

MOUNTED POLICE DODGE SEDAN, 1919. In late April 1919, Captain Sena bought a new Dodge sedan from the J. C. Allen Company in East Las Vegas for $1,264.65. This price included a "high quality" spare tire and repair kit. Sena drove his Dodge until late 1920 when he resigned. Lorenzo Delgado drove the Dodge for a few weeks before the mounted police force was disbanded in February 1921. The Dodge was turned over to the state's adjutant general for his use.

NEW MEXICO MOUNTED POLICE COLLECTION. A large part of the New Mexico Mounted Police Collection was put on public display in July 2000 at the New Mexico State Police headquarters in the Department of Public Safety Building in Santa Fe. Chief Frank R. Taylor accepted the display. He is pictured here holding Captain Fornoff's rifle and talking with the author in his outer office.

THE DISPLAY. The author is shown standing with Sgt. Ron Taylor, New Mexico State Police historian, and agent Norman Rhoads, past president of the New Mexico State Police Association, at the opening of the New Mexico Mounted Police exhibit. The ranger display became part of the visual history of the New Mexico State Police.

Eight

END OF WATCH

REST IN PEACE RANGERS

During the nine years between 1905 and 1913, thirty-seven different men wore the badge of the New Mexico Mounted Police. These men were like peace officers today; they were sons, brothers, husbands, and fathers. They did not think of themselves as heroes or legend-makers. Fred Lambert, the last living territorial mounted policeman, may have pronounced the best eulogy for his brother lawmen: "It was a tough job that needed doing and we boys just done it. Nothing more; nothing less. We got paid to do a job and we done it."

Between 1914 and 1918, hundreds of men carried special commissions as New Mexico Mounted Police in their role as a substitute state militia. In 1918, seventeen men enforced the law as a state policeman. Forty-eight more men wore the mounted police uniform from 1919 to 1921 and continued the traditions established by their predecessors. These too were men of honor and dedication.

Today the men and women who wear the black and gray New Mexico State Police uniform proudly protect the citizens of the Land of Enchantment. Since 1935, these professionals have honored their motto, "Pro Bono Publico—For the Public Good."

Capt. John F. Fullerton's Grave Site. Capt. John F. Fullerton is buried in the Elks' Rest Garden section of Greenwood Memorial Park and Mortuary in San Diego, California. He died in 1928.

Capt. Fred Fornoff's Grave Site. Capt. Fred Fornoff is buried in the Santa Fe National Cemetery at Santa Fe, New Mexico. His grave is number eight in Section T. He died in the military hospital in Sheridan, Wyoming, in November 1935.

Capt. Herb McGrath's Grave Site. The grave of Capt. Herb McGrath is circled in the picture of the McGrath-Baird family plot in the Concordia Cemetery in El Paso. The I-20 highway overpass is seen in the background. The Bairds were McGrath's first wife's family. He died in Silver City in October 1933.

Capt. A. A. Sena's Grave Site. Apolonio A. Sena is buried in Fairview Park Cemetery in Albuquerque, where he died in April 1942.

Capt. Lorenzo Delgado's Grave Site. Lorenzo Delgado is buried in the family plot in the Mount Calvary Cemetery in Las Vegas, New Mexico. He died in Las Vegas in October 1936.

Lt. Cipriano Baca's Grave Site. Cipriano Baca's final resting spot is in the Sunset Memorial Park in Albuquerque. His grave was unmarked until his grandson John P. Amos placed a marker on the grave in the late 1990s. John had last seen his grandfather when he was a small boy visiting with his mother and sisters in September 1935.

Sgt. Robert W. Lewis's Grave Site. Sgt./Lt. Bob Lewis is buried in an unmarked grave in the Lewis family plot in the Socorro Cemetery, Socorro, New Mexico. He died in Magdalena, New Mexico, in August 1950.

Sgt. Will Dudley's Grave Site. This is the marker for the Dudley family in the cemetery at Alamogordo. Will Dudley's wife, Mary Josephine Burleson Dudley, called Josie, and only son, Lenox, are buried here. Three different locations have been suggested as Will Dudley's final resting place.

JOHN J. BROPHY'S GRAVE SITE. John James Brophy, one of Fullerton's Rangers, died of food poisoning at his ranch in Cimarron County, Oklahoma, in June 1916. He is buried in the Clayton Cemetery (New Mexico) in an unmarked site to the right of his son's marked grave. Rosa Duran Brophy's grave is also unmarked. The Brophy graves are within sight of the outlaw Thomas "Blackjack" Ketchem's grave, a tourist site.

OCTAVIANO PEREA'S GRAVE SITE. It is believed that Octaviano Perea is buried in the family plot in the old Lincoln Cemetery in Lincoln, New Mexico, in an unmarked grave. This is a picture of the Perea family marker.

J. B. Rusk's Grave Site. James Battis "Slim" Rusk is buried in the overgrown old mountaintop Chama Cemetery in Chama, New Mexico. He died in January 1912 from pneumonia that developed from a winter cold he contracted while on duty in Colorado bringing a prisoner back to New Mexico.

Grave Site of Frank Vance. Robert Frank Vance is buried between his parents in the pioneer section of Mountain View Cemetery in Cimarron, New Mexico. The site is just across the street from the grave of Fred Lambert. Vance was murdered in January 1912.

FATE AVANT'S GRAVE SITE. Fate Avant is buried in El Paso's Evergreen Cemetery on the other side of I-20 from where Captain McGrath is buried. Avant died in 1940.

ROBERT PUTMAN'S GRAVE SITE. The author made three searches looking for Bob Putman's grave in the Deming Cemetery in Deming, New Mexico. The small concrete marker was finally discovered overgrown by the surrounding grass. Bob died in 1947.

FRED MURRAY'S GRAVE SITE. George Fred Murray is buried in Fairview Park Cemetery in Albuquerque. The former Rough Rider died by his own hand in Grants, New Mexico, in 1955.

M. C. STEWART'S GRAVE SITE. Mills Cicero Stewart died in Carlsbad, New Mexico, in May 1955. He is buried in the Carlsbad Cemetery. The Eddy County Historical Society marked the grave in 1973.

GRAVE SITE OF ALEX STREET. James Alexander Street is buried in Sunnyside Cemetery in Tucumcari, New Mexico. His wife, Lula Belle Berry Street, is buried next to him.

GRAVE SITE OF JIM MCHUGHES. James H. McHughes had served in Europe during the First World War. He is buried in the Santa Fe National Cemetery in Santa Fe. His marker is located on Grave 330, Section O, just a few rows from Captain Fornoff.

J. R. Galusha's Grave Site. J. R. "Chief" Galusha is buried in Fairview Park Cemetery in Albuquerque next to his wife, Effie. Galusha died in 1961. Lullie Howell Bowman Fornoff, Fred Fornoff's wife, rests nearby.

Fred Lambert's Funeral Service. A light rain had fallen the morning the last ranger was laid next to his beloved wife, Katie, on February 9, 1971, following a service in the Cimarron Methodist Church. The service was recorded and later sold as an LP record. Lambert was dressed in a blue suit and wore his special deputy sheriff's badge. The casket was draped in the New Mexico state flag, and his friends were the pallbearers. The author was honored to serve.

THE GRAVE OF FRED LAMBERT. Charles Fredrick Lambert is buried in the pioneer section of Mountain View Cemetery in Cimarron, New Mexico. He and Katie are buried just in front of his mother and father. The grave was first marked with a lawman's star. Today the grave has a marker to match that of his wife.

FRED LAMBERT'S FIRST GRAVE MARKER. The site of Fred Lambert's grave was first marked with a lawman's star. The wood emblem was painted silver and had the words "Lawman 50 Years" burned into it. On the day of the funeral the grave contained a flower arrangement made like a star with the lettering "NMMP" placed on it. Charles Frederick Lambert was the last ranger of the territorial mounted police.

DISCOVER THOUSANDS OF LOCAL HISTORY BOOKS FEATURING MILLIONS OF VINTAGE IMAGES

Arcadia Publishing, the leading local history publisher in the United States, is committed to making history accessible and meaningful through publishing books that celebrate and preserve the heritage of America's people and places.

Find more books like this at
www.arcadiapublishing.com

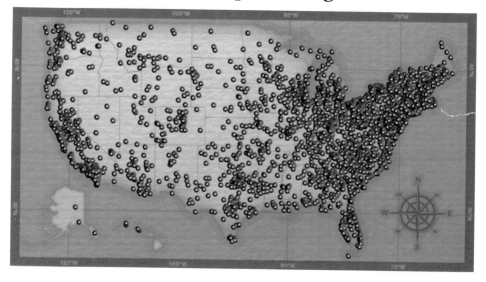

Search for your hometown history, your old stomping grounds, and even your favorite sports team.

Consistent with our mission to preserve history on a local level, this book was printed in South Carolina on American-made paper and manufactured entirely in the United States. Products carrying the accredited Forest Stewardship Council (FSC) label are printed on 100 percent FSC-certified paper.

MADE IN THE USA